MONOGRAPHS OF THE
SOCIETY FOR RESEARCH IN
CHILD DEVELOPMENT

Serial No. 236, Vol. 58, No. 8, 1993

GUIDED PARTICIPATION IN CULTURAL ACTIVITY BY TODDLERS AND CAREGIVERS

Barbara Rogoff
Jayanthi Mistry
Artin Göncü
Christine Mosier

WITH AN AFTERWORD BY
Pablo Chavajay

AND COMMENTARY BY
Shirley Brice Heath

MONOGRAPHS OF THE SOCIETY FOR RESEARCH IN CHILD DEVELOPMENT
Serial No. 236, Vol. 58, No. 8, 1993

CONTENTS

ABSTRACT

ROGOFF, BARBARA; MISTRY, JAYANTHI; GÖNCÜ, ARTIN; and MOSIER, CHRIS-
TINE. Guided Participation in Cultural Activity by Toddlers and Care-
givers. With an Afterword by PABLO CHAVAJAY; and Commentary by
SHIRLEY BRICE HEATH. *Monographs of the Society for Research in Child
Development*, 1993, **58**(8, Serial No. 236).

In this *Monograph*, we examine how toddlers and their caregivers from
four cultural communities collaborate in shared activities. We focus both on
similarities across communities in processes of guided participation—
structuring children's participation and bridging between their understanding and that of their caregivers—and on differences in *how* guided participation occurs. We examine the idea that a key cultural difference entails
who is responsible for learning—whether adults take this responsibility by
structuring teaching situations or whether children take responsibility for
learning through observation and through participating in adult activities
with caregivers' support. We speculate that these two patterns relate to
cultural variation in the segregation of children from adult activities of their
community and in emphasis on formal schooling. The four communities of
our study vary along these lines as well as in other ways: a Mayan Indian
town in Guatemala, a middle-class urban group in the United States, a tribal
village in India, and a middle-class urban neighborhood in Turkey.

In each community, we visited the families of 14 toddlers (aged 12–24
months) for an interview that was focused on child-rearing practices, which
included observations of caregivers helping the toddlers operate novel objects and put on clothes on our request as well as toddlers exploring novel
objects spontaneously during adult activities. Results are based on systematic
analysis of patterns of communication and attention in each family in each
community, combining the tools of ethnographic description, graphic analysis, and statistics.

The findings point to the importance of understanding not only how
children learn through instruction that is managed by adults but also how

they learn through keen observation and participation in adult activities. A major contribution of the study is an analysis of keen observation through sharing attention among complex ongoing events, an approach that was more apparent in the two non-middle-class communities, in which children are minimally segregated from adult activities.

I. INTRODUCTION:
THE CONCEPTS OF GUIDED PARTICIPATION AND CULTURAL UNIVERSALS AND VARIATION

Mi hijo	My son
En un lugar secreto	In a secret place
nuestros antepasados	our ancestors
los ancianos de rostros arrugados	the ones with the wrinkled faces
y cabellos blancos	and white hair
nos dejaron estas palabras:	left us these words:
observa largamente	Look long
sabiamente	and wisely
¿es esto real?	Is this real?
¿es esta la verdad?	Is this the truth?
Ahora	Now
escucha mis palabras	listen to my words
de buen talante	with care
Observa las cosas	Look at things
observa largamente	look long
y sabiamente	and wisely
¿Es esto real?	Is this real?
¿Es esta la verdad?	Is this true?
Así es como debes de trabajar	This is how you must work
y actuar.	and act.

(Gerez, 1984, pp. 34–35)

In this *Monograph,* we examine cultural similarities and variations in how toddlers and their caregivers from four cultural communities collaborate in shared activities. We take the perspective that children's development occurs through active participation in cultural systems of practice in which children, together with their caregivers and other companions, learn and extend the skills, values, and knowledge of their community. This is a process that Rogoff (1990) termed "guided participation," Heath (1989) referred to as "the learner as cultural member," and Lave and Wenger (1991) called "legitimate peripheral participation."

Although there is a great deal of research on children's interaction with their caregivers, most of it is based on middle-class families in the United States or Western Europe. The issue of how much the observed processes are simply a function of the way parents in these specific communities conceive their roles remains open to question. Indeed, cross-cultural observations suggest that there are deep cultural differences in the goals of development, arrangement of childhood activities, and nature of communication between children and their caregivers.

Our study aimed to articulate both similarities and variations in cultural arrangements and communication between children and their caregivers. We expected similarities across quite different communities in processes of guided participation (in terms of bridging between different perspectives on a situation and structuring partners' involvement) because of universal aspects of human communication and shared human efforts. At the same time, we expected cultural variations in how guided participation occurs—especially the means of shared participation and the balance of responsibility for teaching and learning—as well as in the local goals of development, depending on the values, institutions, technologies, and practices of different communities. This introductory chapter provides background for the pattern of cultural similarities and variations in guided participation along with an overview of the concept itself.

We observed how toddlers and caregivers in four cultural communities interacted during routine activities that posed them with typical challenges that involve joint action: operating novel objects and dressing. Our procedures involved interviews and focused observations of child-caregiver interaction that were analyzed through systematic abstraction of patterns that emerged from ethnographic analyses of each family in each community. The observations took place in the context of a child-rearing interview during visits to the families' homes.

The four communities—a Mayan Indian town in Guatemala (San Pedro), a middle-class urban community in the United States (Salt Lake), a tribal village in India (Dhol-Ki-Patti), and an urban middle-class community in Turkey (Keçiören)—were chosen to represent varied social and economic characteristics that we expected to be associated with differing child-rearing arrangements. Most important, these communities were selected to take advantage of the researchers' familiarity with each setting. In all four communities, the researcher responsible for conducting the study spoke at least one of the local languages and had lived or worked previously either in that community or in one similar to it in that nation. In many instances, the researcher had established long-term relationships with the families.

We refer to "communities" or "cultural communities," rather than "cultures" or "nations," so as to avoid the danger of generalizing to national groups from observations of a few people in a single community. Our observations are not necessarily applicable to other communities in the same country or region; hence, we refer to the communities that we have observed by local names.

By "community" we mean a group of people having some common local organization, values, and practices. As Dewey (1916) pointed out, "There is more than a verbal tie between the words common, community, and communication. [People] live in a community in virtue of the things which they have in common; and communication is the way in which they come to possess things in common" (p. 5). It is in the processes of communication that our study looks to understand how children become increasingly involved participants in and contributors to the activities around them. Children's development, we believe, is a creative process of participation in communication and shared endeavors that both derives from and revises community traditions and practices.

We expected *similarity* across the communities in basic processes of guided participation. These processes involve bridging between the participants' interpretations of a situation and the partners' mutual structuring of their involvement, to be evidenced by joint engagement (with variation in who takes a leadership role and in the means of engagement) and by caregivers' and toddlers' joint contributions to managing the activities.

We expected *variation* in the goals promoted for children's development and in associated means of guided participation. Thus, we expected communities to differ in patterns reflecting whether children or adults are responsible for children's learning. One pattern emphasizes adults structuring children's learning by organizing children's attention, motivation, and involvement and by providing lessons removed from the context of ongoing mature activities. Another pattern emphasizes children taking the primary responsibility for learning by managing their own attention, motivation, and involvement through observation and participation in ongoing mature activities, with adults providing more responsive (than directive) assistance. We speculate that community differences in the extent to which children are integrated in adult activities may relate to whether children are primarily responsible for learning or whether adults take responsibility for organizing instruction.

Although we suggest that segregation of children from adult activities (and emphasis on formal schooling) may be important aspects of the two patterns, our study does not isolate this aspect of the communities from other features that are also involved in the patterns. Many other aspects of the organization of the four communities vary with age segregation and extent of schooling—economic resources, family size, maintenance of traditional ways, and urbanization, to name a few. In cultural research, it is impossible to reduce differences between communities to a single variable or two; to do so would destroy the coherence among features that makes it useful to refer to cultural processes.

Our way of handling this issue is to identify a number of aspects of cultural organization that we think are important in the patterns we are attempting to capture and, in addition, to provide a broad description of other features of the communities. We do not mean to imply that age segregation, schooling, or social class "causes" the pattern of differences that we explore in our observations—we do not regard cultural features as independent variables (as in the independent variable/dependent variable design common to psychological research), and we do not seek to establish causality. Rather, we attempt to identify patterns of similarity and differences in guided participation that are associated with cultural practices. We regard an illuminating description of patterns to be the aim of any research.

The four communities included in this study vary in the segregation of children from adult activities in ways that allow us to explore the proposed differences in patterns. San Pedro toddlers could routinely observe their mothers' home-based economic activities (sewing and weaving), and Dhol-Ki-Patti toddlers could observe their mothers working in the fields or in daily paid labor outside the home. In contrast, almost all the middle-class Keçiören toddlers stayed home with mothers whose work did not include economic activity beyond homemaking, and middle-class Salt Lake toddlers either stayed home with homemaking mothers or stayed in settings in which the adults' economic activity was to tend them. In U.S. middle-class communities, children are segregated from the work and social world of adults (Morelli, Rogoff, & Angelillo, 1992).

When their opportunities to observe adult economic activities and adult social relationships are limited, children may have little chance to begin to make sense of the more mature roles of their community (Panel on Youth, 1974; Rogoff, 1990). Without the opportunity to observe and participate in the activities of their communities, young children may need adult guides (e.g., teachers, child-focused parents) to introduce them to mature skills in specialized child-focused settings.

In communities in which children are not segregated from observation and participation in the activities of their elders, however, the responsibility for child development may fall less on those who "raise" the children than on the children themselves "coming up" (the metaphor for child development used in the working-class African-American community studied by Heath, 1983) as they are embedded in the everyday lives and work of their extended family and community.

By examining the coherence of these contrasting patterns—children managing their own learning in ongoing activities and adults organizing instruction for children—we hope to lay the groundwork for a more elaborated picture of systematic variation in how children develop through participation in the activities of their local communities. We investigated whether there is more instructional talk (especially language lessons and peer-like conversations) between caregivers and children in the two communities in which children are segregated from adult activities (Salt Lake and Keçiören) and more reliance on nonverbal symbolic acts (such as gestures and communication using intent gaze expressions, touch, or timing cues) in the two communities in which children are integrated in adult activities (San Pedro and Dhol-Ki-Patti). We also examined differences in the extent to which caregivers provide explanation out of the context of the activity, structure tasks verbally, and manage children's motivation for the task as compared to the extent to which children learn through observation with the aid of caregivers who demonstrate processes, structure tasks primarily nonverbally, and maintain themselves ready to assist when children manifest a need.

In the two communities in which children are integrated in adult activities, we explored the possibility that caregivers and children may attend more keenly to surrounding events—a practice that would facilitate learning through observation—by examining how they attend to events that compete with their current focus of concentration. We expected that paying attention to several ongoing events simultaneously would be more common in communities in which children routinely have an opportunity to observe adult activities and are responsible for learning from observation. Further, we expected that children in San Pedro and Dhol-Ki-Patti would more frequently show involvement that is embedded in a group rather than being engaged in solo or dyadic activity.

To provide background for these expectations, we first give an overview of the concept of guided participation and then review work on similarities and differences in varying cultural communities.

GUIDED PARTICIPATION

We regard children's development as occurring through their active participation in culturally structured activity with the guidance, support, and challenge of companions who vary in skill and status. The concept of guided participation is used in an attempt to keep individual, interpersonal, and cultural processes simultaneously in focus, representing inseparable aspects of whole events in which children and communities develop (Rogoff, in press). The concept provides a perspective on the process by which children develop through their participation in the evolving practices of their community. It stresses guidance—not only in the sense of explicit instruction but also in the sense of development in specific directions that are based on the models of human activity provided by previous generations. It stresses participation in the sense of shared endeavors—not just the focused interaction on which research on communication often centers but also the side-by-side or distal arrangements of activity without co-presence, in which children and their social partners participate while developing their own contributions to, and extensions of, cultural practices.

The concept is not a classification scheme by which one could evaluate whether guided participation is occurring or effective in any particular situation. Rather, it is a perspective through which to view individual, group, and community transformation. It is not limited to the kind of dyadic interactions that have often been the focus of research but instead promotes a focus on systems of relationships (including present and distant partners, groups, and institutions) that must be described in terms of local models of implicit developmental goals—not imposed definitions of the "ideal" goals of development.

The concept of guided participation extends Vygotsky's notion of the "zone of proximal development," in which individual development is regarded as occurring during joint problem solving with people who are more skilled in the use of cultural tools, including inventions such as literacy, mathematics, mnemonic skills, and approaches to problem solving and reasoning (Laboratory of Comparative Human Cognition, 1983; Vygotsky, 1978; Wertsch, 1979). Cole (1985) suggested that, in the zone of proximal development, culture and cognition create each other. Cultural tools and practices are both inherited and transformed by new members of cultural communities. Culture itself is not static; it is formed from the efforts of people working together, using and adapting tools provided by predecessors and in the process creating new ones.

We assume that children advance their understanding in a creative process in which they transform their understanding and become more responsible participants in the practices of their communities as they participate. Learning to coordinate understanding and effort is inherent in observation and participation in social activity because, without some shared understanding, communication and shared activity could not proceed.

The concept of guided participation refers to the process and system of involvement of individuals with others, as they communicate and engage in shared endeavors. It emphasizes children's involvement in structured and diverse relationships and activities with a variety of other people. It includes distal structuring that occurs as children choose (or choose not to) watch television, do chores, or eavesdrop on their parents, as parents extend or limit opportunities by making decisions regarding day care or saving chores until toddlers are asleep, or as communities construct institutions that include or exclude children. The emphasis on tacit and routine forms of communication and on arrangements of children's activities and companions contrasts with the more typical focus on explicit and even didactic dialogue that has characterized Vygotskian theory, with its emphasis on words and academic forms of thought, as well as U.S. research on socialization. This shift of emphasis facilitates an examination of children's development in the context of routine activities of the early years and in cultural communities that are less tied to didactic schooling and the use of academic discourse.

Our aim is to characterize similarities in deep processes of guided participation while specifying differences in how it occurs, with special attention to variations in the contributions of different participants in varying circumstances.

UNIVERSALS AND VARIATIONS IN GUIDED PARTICIPATION

Across differing cultural communities, there are essential similarities as well as differences in child rearing and development. Although it is common to assume that variations across different cultural communities indicate that a phenomenon involves cultural processes whereas similarities across communities demonstrate biological processes, we argue that both variations and similarities involve both types of process (see Rogoff, 1990). Rather than assuming that culture and biology are opposing or even separable factors, we assume that, as a species, humans are biologically social creatures. We concur with Trevarthen's statement that "humans are born with a self-regulating strategy for getting knowledge by human negotiation and co-operative action. . . . Thus socialisation is as natural, innate or 'biological' for a human brain as breathing or walking" (1988, p. 39). Part of our species' heritage is a wide flexibility as well as similarities in cultural arrangements that characterize varying human communities (see also Heath, 1989). Children enter the world embedded in an interpersonal system involving their caregivers and other people who are already involved with societal institutions and technologies.

Universal Processes of Guided Participation

Ethnographic studies of child-rearing practices in other cultural communities support the idea that the general principles of guided participation are widespread around the world. With the guidance of caregivers and companions, children participate in and begin to manage the cultural activities that surround them (Fortes, 1938/1970). Craft apprenticeship in weaving (in Guatemala and Mexico) and in tailoring (in Liberia), learning the skills of cultivation, animal husbandry, hunting, and fishing (in Venezuela), and learning to distinguish between right and left hands for eating during toddlerhood (in India) involve guided participation as novices engage with more skilled practitioners, who may segment and structure the process to be learned, provide guidance during joint activity, and help adjust participation according to increasing skill (Freed & Freed, 1981; Greenfield, 1984; Greenfield & Lave, 1982; Rogoff, 1986; Ruddle & Chesterfield, 1978).

A process of guided participation that we regard as universal is that of bridging to make connections between the known and the new. We believe it to be universal because inherent to communication is a collaborative effort of partners to find a common ground of understanding on which to base their contributions so as to ensure mutual comprehension. Partners initially have somewhat (or greatly) discrepant views of a situation but seek a common perspective or language through which to communicate their ideas; this effort involves a stretch on the part of the participants, making it a developmental process. From the collaboratively constructed common ground, the participants share in thinking as they extend their understanding together.

Children's efforts to participate in ongoing activity involve a stretch in the direction of a more mature definition of the situation and more skilled roles. Children seek connections between old and new situations in their caregivers' emotional cues regarding the nature of a situation and how to handle it, in their interpretations of children's behavior, and in the labels they provide for objects and events that inherently classify similarities across circumstances. Infants as young as 10 months seek information from adults' expressions, proceeding to explore if the adult appears content, but avoiding the situation if the adult appears fearful (Feinman, 1982; Sorce, Emde, Campos, & Klinnert, 1985). Middle-class adults often adapt their contribution to an activity to fit with what they think the children can understand, restructuring the problem to be within children's grasp (Wertsch, 1984).

Although there are likely to be asymmetries in responsibility for adjustment depending on the status of the participants, on the situation, and on societal standards for who is responsible for adjustment (which we discuss later), the phenomenon of seeking shared meaning is in the nature of human communication. Indeed, some authors argue that intersubjectivity between infants and their caregivers is innate—that, from the earliest interactions, infants are involved in the sharing of meaning (Brazelton, 1983; Fernald, 1984; Luria, 1987; Newson, 1977; Trevarthen, Hubley, & Sheeran, 1975).

Thus, in this *Monograph,* we examine the extent to which caregivers and children in all four communities engage jointly in activities to which they each contribute. While we do not expect symmetry in caregivers' and children's roles, we do expect that they will be involved at times in the same activities and that each will provide some management to the direction of events, with caregivers orienting and supporting children's efforts in all four communities.

Cultural Variation in Guided Participation

A central purpose of this *Monograph* is to examine cultural variation in the goals of development and in the means available for children either to observe and participate in culturally important activities or to receive instruction outside the context of skilled activity. We do not regard the cultural variation as being categorical—where each community has only one kind of relationship—but as more in the nature of variations on a theme.

Children in communities that allow or promote observation of adult activities may develop largely through their own initiative, through active observation and gradually increasing participation. In communities that restrict children's access to adult activities through age segregation and compartmentalization of roles, it may be necessary for adults to present children with a watered-down version of adult activities and to work to motivate them to practice these activities out of the context of any obvious purpose. Hence, a major cultural difference may lie in the extent to which caregivers adjust their activities to children as opposed to the extent to which children are responsible for adjusting to and making sense of the adult world.

The bulk of research on the social context of development has been conducted in cultural communities in which explicit instruction from adults—either parents or teachers—is the prototypical socialization situation. This cultural prototype has undoubtedly influenced the field's conceptualization of "socialization," in which children are cast as recipients of instruction that is explicit and organized by adults, with little attention to children's active role in managing their own learning through observation and participation in social activity.

Variation in Goals of Development

In our approach, we attempt to understand development in the context of children's everyday activities and culturally valued goals of development. To study children's communication with their caregivers without attention to cultural variation in goals for development would be like attempting to learn a language without trying to understand the meaning it expresses.

We assume variation in the goals of development rather than a universal endpoint to which all should aspire. In a community in which literacy is a primary means of communication and a requirement for economic success in adulthood, it may be important for preschoolers to learn to attend to the nuances of differences between small, two-dimensional shapes, but such a focus may not matter in other communities, where it may be more important for young children to learn to attend to the nuances of weather patterns or of social cues, to use words cleverly to joust, or to understand the relation between human and supernatural events.

It is easy for Western researchers to focus on skills that are important in our own daily lives and in our communities. In Dewey's (1916, p. 22) words,

> We rarely recognize the extent in which our conscious estimates of what is worthwhile and what is not, are due to standards of which we are not conscious at all. But in general it may be said that the things which we take for granted without inquiry or reflection are just the things which determine our conscious thinking and decide our conclusions. And these habitudes which lie below the level of reflection are just those which have been formed in the constant give and take of relationship with others.

To understand development, we must examine children's involvement in activities in terms of its function in achieving locally valued goals, conscientiously avoiding the arbitrary imposition of our own values on another group; interpreting the activity of people without regard for *their* goals renders observations meaningless. Our study attempts to understand the coherence of what people from varying communities *do* rather than simply determining that non-Western people do *not* do what middle-class Western people do.

We assume that, even in the toddler years, children's participation in activities with their caregivers reflects development toward the goals of functioning within cultural institutions and technologies of skilled social practice in later years. Cultural scholars have argued that basic to cognitive differences across cultural groups are variations in institutions of learning, such as schools and apprenticeships, and their attendant values and technologies (Cole & Griffin, 1980; Heath, 1989; Laboratory of Comparative Human Cognition, 1983; Lave & Wenger, 1991; Rogoff, 1981b; Rogoff, Gauvain, & Ellis, 1984; Scribner & Cole, 1981).

There is evidence that preparation for the use of cultural tools such as literacy begins even before children have contact with the technology in its mature form. Middle-class U.S. parents involve their children in "literate" forms of narrative in preschool discourse, embedding them in a way of life in which reading and writing are integral to communication, recreation, and livelihood (Cazden, 1979; Gundlach, McLane, Stott, & McNamee, 1985; Michaels & Cazden, 1986; Taylor, 1983). Heath (1982, 1983) suggests that middle-class, school-oriented practices for promoting literacy and analytic discourse (such as bedtime stories) in the preschool years relate to later facility in school literacy.

By the early elementary years, children in differing communities become skilled in using the narrative style valued in their community. Michaels and Cazden (1986) found that the narrative style used in "sharing time" by African-American children employed an episodic structure with emphasis on developing themes, yielding narratives judged by African-American adults to be more competent than those of white children. The narrative style used by white children involved tightly structured discourse centered on a single topic, a style that received greater approval from white adults and from teachers and more closely resembled the literate styles that U.S. teachers aim to foster.

In this study, we focus on the guided participation that occurs in communities in which young children develop toward participation in learning institutions that are segregated from mature practice (e.g., in schools) or are expected to develop through participation in surrounding valued adult activities.

Variation in Communication between Children and Adults

Cultural differences in the use of verbal and nonverbal communication have been widely observed (Field, Sostek, Vietze, & Leiderman, 1981; Leiderman, Tulkin, & Rosenfeld, 1977). These differences may relate to cultural differences in children's opportunities and responsibility to observe and participate in culturally important activities instead of receiving instruction by adults outside such contexts (Rogoff, 1990).

Verbal and nonverbal communication.—Greater emphasis on verbal statements and less use of nonverbal cues in instruction appear to characterize communities that involve Western schooling (Jordan, 1977; Richman, LeVine et al., 1988; Rogoff, 1981b, 1982b; Scribner, 1974; Scribner & Cole, 1973). Such differences may relate to cultural values regarding the appropriate forms of communication and use of subtlety and silence. Western researchers' emphasis on talking as the appropriate means of adult-child interaction may reflect a cultural bias that overlooks the information provided by silence, gaze, postural and timing changes, smells, and touch. Middle-class U.S. infants have been characterized as "packaged" babies who do not have direct skin contact with their caregivers (Whiting, 1981), often spend more than a third of their time alone in a room separate from other people, and are held for approximately half the time that Gusii (Kenyan) infants are (Richman, Miller, & Solomon, 1988). Heath (1983) observed that working-class U.S. African-American infants were almost never alone—they were held and carried day and night—and were seldom in the company of only one other person. The separation of mainstream middle-class U.S. infants from other people may necessitate the use of distal forms of communication such as noise; in contrast, children who are constantly in the company of their caregivers may rely more on nonverbal cues such as gaze, gestures, facial expression, and postural changes.

In the present research, we check to see if the usual findings of more talk appear in middle-class communities and examine the possibility that other communities make greater use of communicative gestures and gaze, touch, posture, and timing cues.

Interactional status: Adult and child responsibility for learning.—In some communities, young children are not expected to interact with adults as conversational peers, initiating interactions and being treated as equals in conversation; instead, they may speak when spoken to, replying to informational questions or simply carrying out directions (Blount, 1972; Harkness & Super, 1977; Heath, 1983; Schieffelin & Eisenberg, 1984). Their primary conversational partners may be other children and kin other than parents, such as older cousins, uncles, and grandparents (D. Farran & J. Mistry, personal communication, 1988; Ward, 1971). Whiting and Edwards (1988) noted that, of the 12 cultural groups that they studied, U.S. middle-class mothers ranked highest in sociability with children— interacting with them in a friendly, playful, or conversational way as equals—whereas, in other communities, mothers stressed training or nurturant involvement with children, maintaining authority.

Ochs and Schieffelin (1984) contrasted two cultural patterns of speech between young children and their caregivers. In middle-class U.S. families, caregivers were found to simplify their talk, negotiate meaning with children, cooperate in building propositions, and respond to children's verbal and nonverbal initiations. In Kaluli New Guinea and Samoan families, by contrast, children were expected to adapt to adult situations. Caregivers modeled unsimplified utterances for them to repeat to a third party, directed them to notice others, and built interaction around circumstances to which caregivers wished children to respond. Some communities may use both patterns, as reported by Watson-Gegeo and Gegeo (1986b) in the Kwara'ae (Solomon Islands), where the goal of caregivers to adapt children to the situation was seen as most effectively accomplished by starting at the child's level—although they did not go to the extent of entering into pretend play, which was children's domain (Watson-Gegeo & Gegeo, 1986a).

Whatever the pattern, children participate in activities of their community, but with variation in children's versus caregivers' responsibility to adapt in the process of learning or teaching the more mature practices. In the Mayan community that provided one of the samples of this study, when children interact with adults, it is in the context of participation in adult work. Adults were at least as likely as peers to be interacting with 9-year-olds when the children were involved in household or agricultural work but were almost never engaged with them when children were playing (Rogoff, 1981a). Play is a domain for peer interaction, not adult companionship.

Even in play, the children usually emulated adult roles. These Mayan children learn in the context of participation in adult activities and in play with children; observations confirmed that they seldom received explicit lessons. Adaptation of caregivers to children may be necessary in societies that segregate children from adult activities, thus requiring them to practice skills or learn information outside the mature context of use (Rogoff, 1981a).

In the current study, we examined the idea that middle-class caregivers enter a peer status role with young children by observing whether they and their toddlers are more likely to act as conversational peers and whether they are more likely to enter the role of playmate with toddlers.

Learning through observation and increasing participation.—In societies in which children are integrated in adult activities, children are assured a role in the action, able to observe and eavesdrop on the ongoing processes of life and death, work and play, that are important in their community. As infants, they are often carried wherever their mothers or older siblings go; as young children, they may do errands and roam the community in their free time, watching whatever is going on. They are legitimate peripheral participants (Lave & Wenger, 1991) in the mature activities of their community.

Ward (1971) offered an eavesdropping account of language learning in her description of an African-American community in Louisiana: "The silent absorption in community life, the participation in the daily commercial rituals, and the hours spent apparently overhearing adults' conversations should not be underestimated in their impact on a child's language growth" (p. 37). Small children in that community were not conversational partners with adults, people with whom to "engage in dialogue." They were not encouraged to learn skills in initiating and monopolizing conversation with adults on topics of their own choosing (skills that are useful in middle-class schooling); they held their parents' attention longer if they said nothing. Toddlers learned to sit very still and listen to adults talk—for as long as 3 hours—and to play with other children. Questions between older children and adults involved straightforward requests for information; they were not asked for the sake of conversation or to drill children on topics to which the parents already knew the answers.

Heath (1983) similarly reported that working-class African-American Carolina adults did not treat young children as conversational partners. Rather, the toddlers—who were always in the company of others—moved through phases of echoing and experimenting with variations on the speech around them, at first ignored, but gradually participating in the ongoing discourse. Children were not seen as information givers and were not asked questions for which adults already had an answer. In the words of one grandmother, "Now just how crazy is dat? White folks uh hear dey kids say sump'n, dey say it back to 'em, dey aks 'em 'gain 'n 'gain 'bout things, like they 'posed to be born knowin'" (p. 84). Flexible use of language, adapted to shifting roles and situations, characterized skilled language use in this community. Children were encouraged to be alert to what went on around them in order to see the connections between events. Schieffelin (1990, p. 73) made similar observations of Kaluli language learning:

> Although there is relatively little speech directed to preverbal children, the verbal environment of these children is rich and varied, and from the beginning, infants are surrounded by adults and older children who spend a great deal of time talking to each other. . . . [Toddlers'] actions are referred to, described, and commented upon by members of the household, especially older children, speaking to one another. . . . This talk about the activities and interests of toddlers is available for the toddlers to hear, though it is not addressed to or formulated for them.

In a Mayan community in Mexico, Gaskins and Lucy (1987) found that children's lower status and freedom to observe meant that they had access to events unavailable to adults. They provided extra eyes and ears for their mothers, who stayed at home and extracted information regarding village events from the children. Mothers' questions about events guided the children regarding what aspects of events are significant.

Children who are not conversational partners of adults may be inexperienced in the pattern of discourse used in school, but they become proficient in the language and other skills of their community. They can be responsible for much of the work of socialization themselves, by watching their elders and gradually becoming more centrally involved, in a process that Benedict (1955) called "continuity of cultural conditioning." With such opportunities to observe ongoing activity and to give a hand when necessary, children from many communities begin to participate in chores and other activities from age 3 or 4, when they begin to see what to do, and assume responsibilities for child, animal, and house care by age 5 or 7 (Rogoff, 1981a; Rogoff, Sellers, Pirotta, Fox, & White, 1975; Ward, 1971; Whiting & Edwards, 1988). Their roles grow, and their opportunities to practice are amplified by their interest in participation and by caregivers' setting them tasks that are within their capabilities and guiding their contributions in the context of joint activity.

For example, Guatemalan Mayan mothers reported that children learn to make tortillas through observing and participating, with mothers providing support in the context of participation (Rogoff, 1990). Toddlers observe their mothers making tortillas and attempt to follow suit; mothers give them a small piece of dough to use and facilitate their efforts by rolling the dough in a ball and starting the flattening process. The child's tortilla is cooked and eaten by family members. As the child becomes more skillful, the mother adds pointers and demonstrations about holding the dough in a position that facilitates smooth flattening. Children can both witness the outcome of their own efforts and contribute to making meals.

Reports of learning by Pueblo Indians and Japanese parents stress children's role as "apprentice" to more experienced members of the community, with observation and verbal explanation being given in the context of involvement in the process that is being learned (John-Steiner, 1984; Kojima, 1986; see also Cazden & John, 1971). Children have access to many aspects of adult life and the freedom to choose how and with whom to participate; adults give them the opportunity to observe and demonstrate the task, expecting children to watch and gradually learn.

Efforts to aid children in learning may thus vary in terms of children's responsibility to observe and analyze activities as opposed to caregivers' responsibility to decompose the task and motivate children. Dixon, Levine, Richman, and Brazelton (1984) noted that Gusii (Kenyan) mothers gave their 6–36-month-old infants the responsibility for learning. They used clear "advance organizers" in instruction, often modeling the expected performance in its entirety, and appeared to expect that, if the child attended to it, the task would be completed exactly as specified. This contrasted with the efforts of American mothers, who took the responsibility for teaching and making their babies learn by attempting to arouse their interest and shaping their behavior step by step, providing constant encouragement and refocusing. A central purpose of the present research is to investigate cultural variation in children's efforts to observe and in adults' means of supporting children's learning.

In this study, we examined the possibility that explanations out of context and caregivers' attempts to motivate children's engagement may be more prevalent in the two middle-class communities whereas demonstration and caregivers' attempts to support children's engagement may be more prevalent in the other two communities. In order to explore the process of observing, we also examined whether caregivers and children attend exclusively to one focus of attention or whether they share their attention by alternating among or even attending simultaneously to several events that compete with their current focus of concentration. We expected that people who rely more extensively on observation in learning (as in San Pedro and, we assume, Dhol-Ki-Patti) may be keen observers who maintain attention to several events at once.

Cultural variation in embeddedness in a group.—The sort of intimate face-to-face mother-infant interaction that has been the subject of much developmental research may be very atypical in cultural settings where infants are less oriented toward their parents as primary social partners and instead function as members of the community with less individual, dyadic focus.

In some communities, supervision of children is the responsibility of the whole community, without the need for any particular adult to be dedicated to devoting attention to them (Heath, 1989; Rogoff, Mistry, Göncü, & Mosier, 1991; Ward, 1971).

Mothers in many communities commonly hold their infants facing away from them (Heath, 1983; Martini & Kirkpatrick, 1981; Sostek et al., 1981). Martini and Kirkpatrick (1981) noted that Marquesan (South Pacific) mothers appeared strained and awkward when asked to interact face to face with their babies because babies are usually held facing outward and encouraged to interact with and attend to people other than their mothers, consistent with a cultural value of embeddedness in a complex social world. Marquesan mothers actively arrange infants' social interactions with others; if babies appear to get self-absorbed, mothers interrupt such absorption and urge attention to the broader social environment. Similarly, Kaluli mothers encourage even newborns to interact with others, facing their babies outward so that they both see and are seen by others in their social group. Mothers often face infants toward older children and speak for them in a special high-pitched register to which the older children are expected to respond as conversation (Schieffelin, 1991). Kaluli children's involvement in multiparty conversations that go in many directions may relate to their learning how to track many things simultaneously.

Following this line of thought, we investigated whether San Pedro and Dhol-Ki-Patti toddlers were more likely than toddlers in the two middle-class communities to engage in multiparty interactions within a group. We think that this could relate to differences in the way they share their attention among competing events, which we speculate may be important in communities that emphasize observation as a means of learning.

STRUCTURE OF THE MONOGRAPH

To summarize our expectations, in all four communities, we expected caregivers and children to engage in joint activities frequently, with shared management of the direction of events and with caregivers orienting and supporting children's efforts.

We expected to find differences in goals of development, means of communication, and the balance of responsibility, with adults taking responsibility for organizing children's learning in the two middle-class communities and children taking responsibility for learning—with their caregivers' responsive assistance—in the other two communities. We expected more talk and explanation referring out of the context of current activity in the middle-class communities and greater use of demonstration and of communicative gestures as well as gaze, touch, posture, and timing cues in the other two communities. We expected middle-class caregivers to act as conversational peers and as playmates with their toddlers and to attempt to motivate children's involvement more frequently and non-middle-class caregivers to attempt to support children's own efforts more frequently. We expected that people who rely more extensively on observation in learning (in San Pedro and, we assumed, Dhol-Ki-Patti) are likely to share their attention among several events at once and to engage in multiparty interactions within a group; engaging in solitary action or dyadic relations with attention to one event at a time was expected to characterize attention in the two middle-class communities.

The next chapter describes our procedures for data collection, and the following chapter is devoted to explaining the method that we used to abstract patterns from our observations, which is likely to be unfamiliar to many readers. Pattern abstraction (derived from Rogoff & Gauvain, 1986) began with close ethnographic description of the observations of each family in each community, attempting to portray the meanings of the events in terms that capture local, family goals and practices. Through the intimate knowledge that develops from such description, the team articulated the expectations that we have reviewed in this introduction and developed specific categories of analysis that we felt portrayed the crucial similarities and differences across communities in terms that could abstract across the specifics of the observations while still maintaining the essence. This was a long process of dialogue among the four researchers, each representing personal knowledge of a different community, deriving from the close descriptions of the observations and from familiarity with the community. Thus, we systematically abstracted from our close descriptions to devise a common language to describe and compare the patterns of guided participation of toddlers and caregivers in the four communities. Our ideas regarding the patterns as well as how to articulate them in coding categories emerged from immersion in close analysis of the data.

Chapter IV presents a comparison of the patterns observed in San Pedro and Salt Lake, the analysis that formed the basis for the respective analyses for Dhol-Ki-Patti (Chap. V) and for Keçiören (Chap. VI). Our decision to treat the data from Dhol-Ki-Patti and from Keçiören as separate extensions of the San Pedro and Salt Lake analyses is intended to help readers understand the patterns of the variables within each community. Our aim was to examine the coherence of the cultural patterns formed by the complex of variables within each community, not to look at culture as an independent variable or to attend to differences variable by variable. We also wanted to structure our account in a way that helps readers follow our methods. The dialogue between researchers "representing" the four different communities was an indispensable tool in developing our coding scheme and understanding the results; we think that the voices of expertise regarding interpretation for each community are more intact when we follow the community-by-community organization to include the Dhol-Ki-Patti and Keçiören analyses as extensions of the San Pedro and Salt Lake findings.

In the final chapter, we synthesize our findings and discuss directions that we suggest can fruitfully extend the results of this study, especially in the areas of how children learn to observe, how children learn through observation and participation, and how cultural variation and similarities can be used as resources for creative approaches to education in our nation.

II. PROCEDURES USED IN DATA COLLECTION

The interpretation of activities in varying cultural communities requires understanding the local meaning and purpose of the activities observed and how the immediate observations fit into broader cultural activity. We attempted to gather and interpret our data in ways that fit with local practices and understandings.

In this study, we focused on child-caregiver interaction in everyday problem situations—operating novel objects and putting on a shirt—that occurred in the course of a videotaped child-rearing interview similar to those common in ethnographic studies of children's lives (e.g., Hilger, 1966; Whiting et al., 1966). Caregiver-child interaction was observed both when the child was the focus of adult attention and when the caregiver was primarily involved in adult conversation. The setting approximates a visit to the home by a friendly acquaintance who has a special interest in the particular child. It is a public situation, focusing on child rearing.

Our aim was to understand the internal coherence of within-community patterns by seeking cross-community similarities and differences in children's socially organized problem-solving activities rather than to make simple contrasts of a variable or two across communities. We wanted to illuminate the complex organization of sociocultural activity, not to establish causality among variables or rankings of communities. Rather, we viewed the opportunity to make similar observations in varying communities as a chance to understand commonalities and variations in patterns of children's guided participation in cultural activity and hence better to understand the cultural nature of all children's development.

Our analysis is thus based on ethnographic approaches in two senses. Our lengthy involvement with the communities and study of local practices involve ethnography at the level of understanding the coherence of community practices, especially as they relate to children's lives. Our close description of the observations made during the visits entails an ethnographic approach (sometimes referred to as microethnography) in which the aim is to understand the meaning of what is observed in small moments of cultural activity and to relate these observations to cultural institutions, practices, and traditions. Our pattern abstraction relied on close ethnographic analysis of the observations during our visits, which were selected and interpreted as windows on cultural activity on the basis of our broader ethnographic understanding of the communities.

Our procedures for gathering data, including some background information on the selection of the communities and samples, are presented in this chapter, and our methods for the analysis of the observations are presented in the next one. Characteristics of the families and more detailed background information on each community are given in the chapters describing the patterns of guided participation observed in each community.

CULTURAL SETTINGS AND SELECTION OF FAMILIES

Selection of Research Sites

The research took place in four communities—involving Guatemalan Mayan, Indian tribal, urban middle-class Turkish, and urban middle-class U.S. families—chosen to obtain variation in the circumstances of children's lives as well as to take advantage of the investigators' familiarity with these communities. The Guatemalan town had been studied over a period of 18 years (with 2 years in residence to conduct ethnographic and psychological research) by Rogoff, who is familiar with the local Mayan language and with the individuals who participated in the study. The Indian village is one in which Mistry (a native of India who is fluent in Hindi, a language closely related to dialects used in the village) had friends and relatives working. The Turkish setting includes relatives of Göncü's (he is a native of Turkey, fluent in the local languages). The U.S. site was the one in which all four authors resided when we began our collaboration.

In each community, the sample consists of a group of families that are associated through overlapping social networks and kinship and consequently are somewhat homogeneous in values and child-rearing practices. As noted earlier, the findings from one village or neighborhood should not be generalized to the nation at large; the aim of the study was to use variation among communities to characterize processes of children's involvement in cultural activity, not to characterize nations.

The Research Team

Two unusual and critically important features of this study are the common perspective of the investigators and their familiarity with the communities studied. The investigators had worked together for over a year using the same general perspective before beginning to gather data, and, at each site, the research was carried out by one of us with the aid of a local resident who assisted in making contact with families and in running the interview. In Dhol-Ki-Patti, Mistry was accompanied by a local person who was fluent in the local dialect and could aid her in understanding a long, complicated reply if she requested. In Keçiören, a local resident accompanied Göncü to run the camera. In San Pedro, Rogoff relied on a local assistant to translate the questions that she posed in Spanish into the local Mayan language; however, she could understand most of the responses made in Mayan without translation, and some of the parents preferred conversing in Spanish (and thus directly with her). Mosier was also present at the San Pedro interviews as a camera operator. In Salt Lake, two researchers—usually Rogoff and Mosier—visited each home, sometimes accompanied by one of the other authors or an assistant.

Selection of Specific Families

In each community, we observed 14 families. Since, by the time 12 or so families had been visited, each research team felt confident that observed patterns would recur in the next families visited, we believe that observations of 14 families are sufficient to derive patterns that are reasonably general to the community, ironing out the variations due to the particulars of each family's situation.

The decision to study 12–24-month-olds was based on the more observable and frequent interactions with adults than would occur were the focus on older children. The first two years of life involve more intensive caregiving and provide an opportunity for richer observation of socialization than later years. The caregiver is frequently the child's mother, while, after about 3 years, there is more variation in who provides care, with other adults and siblings often taking over responsibility for the child (Weisner & Gallimore, 1977) or children becoming responsible for themselves for long periods (Mosier, Rogoff, & Chavajay, 1992). In addition, there are more similarities across communities in the challenges to be met at this age (e.g., dressing, learning how objects work) than at older ages, when they diverge more according to community practices (such as varying emphasis on schooling). Our interest in studying problem solving led to a focus on the second rather than the first year of life.

There are difficulties associated with studying toddlers, however. One is that, in many cultures (including the Mayan and Indian samples), babies have traditionally been considered especially vulnerable to the effects of evil eye and other dangers and are often protected from strangers (see the difficulties encountered by Brazelton, 1977). Gaining rapport with toddlers was facilitated in this study by the fact that the investigator was familiar with the community and often acquainted with the families.

The selection of the 14 families in each community occurred through the researcher's familiarity with families with a child aged 12–24 months or through participants' suggestions regarding other families with a child of the appropriate age. The average age of the children in each of the four communities was 17 months, with a range of 12–22 months in San Pedro, 12–23 months in Salt Lake, 12–24 months in Dhol-Ki-Patti (where ages were estimated because they are not kept track of), and 12–25 months in Keçiören. We included an equal number of girls and boys distributed similarly through this age range in each community except Keçiören, where the sample consisted of eight girls and six boys.

A notable difference across communities was the children's birth order, which reflected differences in family size in each community. In San Pedro, four children were firstborn, two secondborn, three thirdborn, and five fourth- through eighthborn. In Sale Lake, seven children were firstborn, four secondborn, and three thirdborn. In Dhol-Ki-Patti, four children were firstborn, four secondborn, two thirdborn, and four fourth- through seventhborn. In Keçiören, nine children were firstborn, four secondborn, and one thirdborn.

In San Pedro, Salt Lake, and Keçiören, each investigator sought the kind of variety in family size, mother's education, and economic resources that reflects the variations prevalent in the community; the Dhol-Ki-Patti sample included almost all toddlers in the village. Although it was not our aim to sample randomly within a population or to generalize to the characteristics of the population as a whole, our sampling was somewhat representative of the variations in the specific communities studied. Descriptions of family education and economic resources and other background information are presented in the chapters describing the results for each community. Here we describe the procedures for recruitment in each site.

Guatemalan Mayan town (San Pedro).—A decade before this study began, Rogoff had worked with 180 San Pedro children in several studies of cognitive development and family background. She came to know many of their families well—having conducted home visits and up to nine other sessions with the children—and remained in contact through the years. The participants for the present study were recruited from these families; most were the children, siblings, or nieces or nephews of the children who had been studied a decade before (a few came from other families that were well known to Rogoff). Thus, Rogoff entered the homes not as a stranger but as a familiar foreigner, greeted with affection and reminiscences about shared experiences. Although the toddlers did not themselves know the investigator, they seemed to pick up from their families that this was a familiar and welcome visitor. This is especially important because, in this community, strangers are sometimes used to threaten toddlers into obedience (e.g., "If you don't behave, that stranger will give you a shot!"). The children appeared quite accepting of the visit; their mothers often commented that the baby was usually more shy with other visitors than with us.

U.S. middle-class families (Salt Lake).—The U.S. families were recruited through neighborhood, work, and child-care connections they had with the investigators or through previous participation in another study. Although the investigators were personally known to only a few of the families, the mothers and children were interested in the study and seemed comfortable with the visits.

Indian tribal village (Dhol-Ki-Patti).—A family friend who worked as the extension specialist from the State Department of Rural Development introduced Mistry to the senior teacher who ran the elementary school in the village and had records of the number and approximate ages of the children in each family (since it was part of her responsibility to encourage parents to send their children to school). This teacher recruited some of the families, who in turn introduced the investigator to other families. She had a higher social status than the residents of the village because of her role as teacher, but she was also familiar to the families. In most cases, they participated because the teacher (who occasionally came along as an assistant) asked them to do so. The presence of visitors may have made mothers more reserved than usual in interacting with their toddlers. For instance, they were likely to be less playful or affectionate with their toddlers because such expressions are regarded as inappropriate for public situations. The toddlers varied in the degree of ease they seemed to feel, from shy to at ease.

Turkish middle-class neighborhood (Keçiören).—This Turkish neighborhood is where Göncü grew up, and most of the families were familiar to him. One parent in the study is his cousin, and three others are childhood friends. The other families were acquainted with the Turkish research assistant, with Göncü, and with the initial participants. The parents and grandparents participated in the study with enthusiasm, pride, and trust, as they regarded it as an effort of a successful "son" or "brother" who was going to make a statement about them. They introduced Göncü to the children with reference to their shared past or to Göncü's status as an academic, referring to him as the children's older brother or uncle, a common term for nonrelatives or relatives ("See, Uncle is a professor. When you grow up, you'll be one also. Right, son?").

THE INTERVIEW/OBSERVATION PROCEDURE

Setting Up the Context

In each culture, the interview occurred in the family home or court-yard, with the mother and toddler present along with any other family members or neighbors who happened to be there. All families had been contacted in advance and asked if they were interested in participating and were told that the purpose of the study was to learn from the differences and similarities across the four cultures in how children are raised. A convenient time was set up for the visits, and at the visit each family was given a gift for the child.

We adjusted the visits in several ways to make them culturally appropriate across the four sites. One arrangement that varied was the length and number of visits; however, all the children were visited for a total of about an hour and a half. All visits were completed in one session in San Pedro, as were most in Salt Lake. In Dhol-Ki-Patti, most children were visited two or three times over a few days, so as not to disrupt the mother's day unduly, and so that families had a chance to become comfortable with the visits. In Keçiören, a preliminary visit was devoted to obtaining information on family background and child characteristics.

The nature of the gifts also varied across communities. Although the gifts were generally worth about $7.00, this amount represents much more in some settings than in others: in San Pedro and Dhol-Ki-Patti, this was at least a week's wage; in Keçiören, it was less than a day's wage but several days' food; and, in Salt Lake, it was about an hour's wage. The nature of the gifts was adjusted to the local context: In San Pedro, the families were given a large towel and a shirt for the child and, in Dhol-Ki-Patti, a bucket and a mug for bathing the child. In Salt Lake, the children received an attractive children's book and, in Keçiören, a monetary gift as the child's "first earnings," which one father said he would frame and another planned to use to open the child's own bank account. In each setting, the gifts were seen as generous and appropriate. In the two non-middle-class settings, however, they were household necessities, and, in the two middle-class settings, they involved private property for the child that could be seen as investments for the child's future (earnings in Keçiören, learning in Salt Lake).

The mothers in the different settings varied in their perception of the purpose of the situation. In San Pedro, mothers saw it as a friendly visit of an acquaintance interested in child development and skills. In Dhol-Ki-Patti and Salt Lake, the mothers seemed to regard the visit as a pleasant social obligation to help the local schoolteacher or the researcher by answering questions. In Keçiören, women treated the session as an opportunity to show their best, treating the visitors as guests by offering coffee or tea and cookies and sometimes a meal, and demonstrating their children's skills, toys, and newest clothes. (A friend of one of the Turkish grandmothers observed this situation and asked, with humor in her tone, "This is an international contest, Artin, isn't it?")

In San Pedro, the interviews were videotaped in their entirety and followed a script involving the presentation of the gift to the mother and some cookies to the child; some small talk; obtaining information about family background and the child's daily routine, companions, and play; the introduction of novel objects; questions regarding chores and socialization for appropriate behavior; questions regarding the child's health, birth, and achievements and the parents' aspirations for the child; drawing a map of the household; presenting a new shirt or sweater and having the mother help the toddler get it on; and observing the child with a drink and a snack. If any of these topics occurred spontaneously out of sequence, they were taken up when they arose.

In Salt Lake, the same script was followed, except that the gift came at the end rather than at the beginning of the session, in order to avoid having the book become a focal point of the interactions.

In Dhol-Ki-Patti, the visits began with the presentation of the gifts and then the interview, in the same order as in San Pedro, but with the novel objects sometimes introduced earlier if the baby's mood seemed to call for diversion. A few of the interviews were not videotaped in order to accustom families to the visit gradually and also because of a shortage of tape.

In Keçiören, the families were videotaped only while responding to the researchers' requests to have the child handle the novel objects, demonstrate social games, eat something, and be dressed; the gift was presented at the end of the visit. The interview was not videotaped (owing to shortage of tape); it either preceded or followed the taping of demonstrated activities, depending on the child's mood and on whether any of the activities to be videotaped occurred spontaneously (e.g., dressing).

Interview Topics and Activities

The following paragraphs describe the main interview questions and how they fit with the requests that the caregiver get the child to operate the novel objects and demonstrate dressing, feeding, and social games. The interviews often followed this order, with the open-ended questions adjusted to the flow of conversation to allow a natural order.

Background family information.—The information collected included names of family members, their approximate age and educational background, and their work. We asked how long the family had lived in this neighborhood, whether they had relatives living nearby, and whether they had lived or visited in another culture. We asked their religion and obtained information on the nature of their material possessions, including whether they owned their home and its size, and we sketched a map of the household.

Caregiving and social network.—We asked who helped the mother with the toddler (kin, paid baby-sitters, day-care center) and what age and type of playmate the child had (parents, siblings, neighbors, play groups, day care).

Daily routine.—We inquired about the toddler's *feeding* routine, such as whether the toddler handled feeding implements independently and whether the toddler still nursed (and, if not, when weaned). (We later suggested that the baby have something to eat—if this had not occurred spontaneously—in order to observe the toddler's and caregiver's interactions around the problems presented by handling local feeding implements. However, we decided not to analyze these data because our requests were very different in the four communities, resulting in full meals in one community and small snacks or a drink in others.)

We asked whether the toddler participated in *dressing* and how the child learned to help in the process. (At the end of the session, if dressing had not occurred spontaneously, we offered a shirt or requested that the caregiver change the child in order to observe how the toddler helps.)

We asked when, where, and with whom the toddler slept at night and during the day and made a map of the *sleeping* arrangements. We asked whether there was a bedtime routine (e.g., story, rocking, lullaby, games, brushing teeth) or security objects (pacifier, teddy bear, blanket) and whether the toddler fell asleep alone or was held until asleep.

Play and social games included questions about what sort of play/social games the toddler enjoyed (e.g., peek-a-boo, finger games, hiding) and with whom and with what toys and household objects the toddler liked to play. (We requested that the mother encourage the child to demonstrate a game sometime later in the session. A separate paper analyzing the toddlers' play during the sessions is being prepared [Göncü, Mistry, & Mosier, in progress].)

Novel objects.—At this point in the interview, we presented the novel objects, asking the caregiver to get the child to operate them. Eight novel objects were presented. The five novel objects marked with an asterisk are the ones that became the focus of our observational analyses of the novel objects (for photographs of these five novel objects, see Fig. 1):

*A metal embroidery hoop with handles to detach the two rings;
*A pencil box with a latchable sliding lid and pictures on the top;
 A set of nesting dolls;

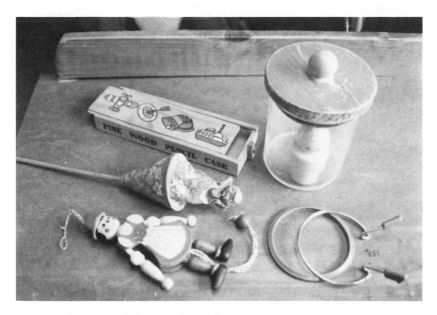

Fig. 1.—The novel objects: pencil box, jar with peewee doll inside, embroidery hoop, jumping jack, and cone puppet.

*A wooden jumping-jack doll that dances when a dangling string is pulled;
*A clear plastic jar and lid with a small doll inside;
A wooden cigarette case with a sliding, wrap-around lid;
*A peek-a-boo puppet animal mounted on a stick that is used to push it in and out of a cone; and
A plastic latching videocassette case.

There were also a few additional objects presented in one or another community.

Chores.—We asked whether the toddler tried to help the caregiver around the house and whether the caregiver showed the toddler how to help. In San Pedro and Salt Lake, these questions led to a request that the caregiver get the child to make tortillas or patties with a ball of Play-Doh that we presented and to take care of a baby doll that we presented. (These activities, along with the interactions involving the nesting doll, were analyzed for a subset of the San Pedro and Salt Lake samples in a previous paper [Rogoff, Mosier, Mistry, & Göncü, in press], which served to help us develop our coding scheme and analyses; results were consistent with those of this *Monograph*.)

Socialization for proper behavior.—We asked the caregivers how they taught the child what he or she is allowed to do and how to treat others with proper manners and how they encouraged the toddler to eliminate properly.

Health and birth.—We asked the caregivers where the child was born, whether there were birth complications or the child had ever suffered from a serious illness, and whether any of their children had died.

Development and aspirations.—We asked whether the child was growing and developing at the rate the caregiver expected and about the child's current progress in walking and talking and whether caregivers did anything to encourage these developments. We also asked what they imagined their child might turn out like as an adult.

Background information on the children obtained in the interviews (e.g., birth order) was presented in our description of the selection of specific families. The remaining interview information is summarized at the beginning of each of Chapters IV–VI, combined with more general ethnographic information gained from familiarity with the communities and families. Although some interview questions proved ambiguous (and were dropped from the analysis), the replies to most of them were clear and are reported in the three results chapters, either in terms of the prevalence of differing practices in each community or as general descriptions of what was learned from conversations during the interviews.

III. ANALYSIS STRATEGY FOR THE OBSERVATIONS

In this chapter, we first discuss our approach to data analysis and interpretation, which relies on systematically abstracting patterns derived from ethnographic analysis of the videotaped visit to each family. We then describe in detail the stages of analysis, which proceeded from (a) ethnographic description to (b) developing a common language for discussing the cases that would capture individual and cultural variation to (c) coding the observations according to the categories of that common language to (d) analyzing the patterns of guided participation graphically and statistically and preparing them for communication to readers.

Our approach contrasts with others that focus on individuals as the unit of analysis, with the behavior of individuals conceived as separate from and related mechanistically to that of other people and to cultural characteristics (see Altman & Rogoff, 1987; Pepper, 1942; Rogoff, 1982a). Our view focuses on activities rather than individuals as the unit of analysis and assumes that developmental processes of individuals simultaneously constitute and are channeled by social and cultural processes (see Rogoff, in press).

We combine ethnographic analysis of the interactions in each family in each community with systematic abstractions from these single-case analyses to analyze patterns appearing across multiple cases (see Rogoff & Gauvain, 1986). We believe that approaches that focus on the behaviors of individuals, defined *separately* from each other, arbitrarily separate the partners' contributions to whole dynamic events. The analysis of patterns of activity considers the mutually constituting actions of the participants in the context of the changing meaning and function of an event rather than imposing a static framework on the participants' actions.

Analyses that arbitrarily separate the contributions of each participant in the interaction make it difficult to capture the meaning of their actions. The separation of individuals' behaviors from the interactional context requires each event to be coded in terms of surface characteristics rather than in terms of the purposes that actions serve for the participants. In an ongoing interaction, a given act may mean something different at one point in the interaction than at another, but a static code that separates the behaviors of the participants has to assign a behavior the same meaning wherever it occurs, ignoring the fact that, in communication, the meaning of an action changes as circumstances change. For example, a mother's question "What do you think goes next?" means one thing if a child has just handled a similar problem with confidence but quite another if it follows a succession of errors.

In addition, any action may serve several alternative or simultaneous purposes (Leont'ev, 1981). For example, a mother's glance at her child may function to maintain her child's attention, evaluate the child's understanding, or maintain her social status relative to the child, among other purposes. The coding of an individual participant's behavior independent of the other participants' behaviors and of preceding events removes the communicational context and meaning, missing the processes involved in participants' management of communication and shared activity.

Attempting to interpret interaction from coded superficial behavior of independently analyzed individuals requires a large step of inference regarding the meaning of the data when the coding does not directly examine the meaning or purpose of the participants in the activity. Often, the eventual interpretation of such data relies on unchecked guesses based on preconceptions or haphazard observation of events (during piloting or running the study) before they were reduced to coded behaviors. Adamson and Bakeman (1982) noted that, if researchers "attempt to discern the organization of infants' interactions with their environment . . . [by coding] occurrences of discrete behavior patterns, interobserver agreement may be high but analyses of such frequency count data may leave them with a sense that little has been retained about the dynamics of the interactive process" (p. 1). Achieving reliability of coded behaviors thus does not solve the problem of trustworthiness of conclusions. Although measures of reliability ensure that several observers independently agreed on how to code a specific behavior, the basis of the researcher's interpretation of the pattern of data is more readily available if the coded variables address the level of meaning that the researcher uses in interpreting the data.

Werner (1954, pp. 8–9) argued for the necessity of analysis of meaningful wholes:

> If it is impossible to derive the totality from a synthesis of the elements, it follows that the only course left is to seek an explanation in the totality itself. The entire problem is now reversed. The elements are not precedent to the whole, but the whole, as a basic entity, is the precursor of its component parts. . . . It is not the concept of "creative synthesis" but that of "creative analysis" which leads to fruitful results. The component members of a mass are dependent parts of this mass,

which represents the real, living unity. The single man as a member of a generic unity possesses characteristics which are his because of his integration within a totality, and are intelligible only in terms of this totality.

Ethnographic and related analyses focus on the meaning and purpose of the participants in events, often analyzing a few cases in depth (see Bremme & Erickson, 1977; Cazden, Cox, Dickinson, Steinberg, & Stone, 1979; Cicourel, 1974; Fox, 1988; Gardner & Rogoff, 1982; Jacob, 1987; McDermott, Gospodinoff, & Aron, 1978; Mehan, 1979; Rogoff & Gardner, 1984). Such analyses are based on the idea that participants in social interaction usually provide explicit evidence to each other regarding the meaning of their actions, informing each other of their intentions through jointly created discourse and action and clarifying ambiguities. This evidence is essential to the achievement of understanding between participants, and it also provides researchers with evidence regarding the meaning of actions (Shotter, 1978). As McDermott et al. (1978, p. 247) note, "We can use the ways members have of making clear to each other and to themselves what is going on to locate to our own [the researchers'] satisfaction an account of what it is that they are doing with each other. In fact, the ways they have of making clear to each other what they are doing are identical to the criteria which we use to locate ethnographically what they are doing."

Rigorous ethnographic researchers provide checks on their interpretations by presenting rich transcript material and by balancing a small sampling of individuals with more intensive analysis of the sample of observed behavior in order to examine all relevant data. This contrasts with research that involves statistical methods with large samples, in which most of the variation observed is regarded as random and relegated to the error term. Mehan (1979) emphasizes the aim of constructing a model that accounts for the organization of each and every relevant instance rather than regarding anomalies as random error.

Reliability and validity are handled differently in ethnographic than in conventional psychological research (Guba & Lincoln, 1982; LeCompte & Goetz, 1982). In conventional research, the investigator trains several observers to a criterion of agreement regarding how to label what is seen, reports the level of agreement on labels, and bases the interpretation of the data on the labels assigned by those observers. However, the fact that several observers can achieve consensus on what to call a behavior does not make their label "true." It simply means that, if another person were similarly trained (enculturated), he or she would likely call that behavior by the same label. Hence, objectivity is no more than shared subjectivity, in conventional approaches just as in all others. All accounts are interpretations; they vary only in the basis on which they are made. Cicourel (1974) pointed out that

31

researchers cannot avoid interpretation in *any* kind of research because they must rely on knowledge of the context and of norms for behavior in order to recognize the relevance of the observed behavior for the theory being tested. Since ethnographic approaches often interpret the data closer to the observed events, they make the evidence for their interpretations of the event more explicit and subject to the reader's scrutiny, providing a different test of reliability. The reader is frequently given excerpts to check the investigator's interpretation of instances, and, in some cases, transcripts of the entire corpus of raw data are made available for public examination (e.g., Green & Wallat, 1979; Mehan et al., 1976).

Some ethnographic approaches examine generalities or patterns in a variety of similar cases (i.e., individuals, dyads, classrooms, events) while attempting to maintain the meaning of individual actions in their context (see Mehan, 1979; Wellman & Sim, 1990). Functional pattern analysis, suggested by Rogoff and Gauvain (1986), is such an approach. It served as the basis of our analyses and can be summarized as follows:

1. Functional pattern analysis focuses on the unfolding development of purposive acts within ongoing events. Categories are functionally defined as they relate to the purposes of the event as a whole rather than as involving superficial behaviors independently defined and separated from their context.

2. The contributions of participants are examined in the context of those of other individuals; this differs from the traditional separation of individuals' behaviors to code them without reference to the efforts of others or to the development of joint activity over the course of an event. Evidence for constructing an account of the participants' goals is available in the communication of participants (including the researcher).

3. Patterns are analyzed with statistical methods as well as with examination of graphic arrays that allow tracking across multiple variables to examine patterns of interrelations and to account for anomalous or similar cases. Anomalies are pursued as informative for the results as a whole, and raw data are referred to in the attempt to account for them and to substantiate general patterns by looking within cases. Statistical approaches, examination of graphic arrays, and ethnographic analyses of individual cases supplement each others' vantage points for interpreting the data.

This approach to analyzing data is similar to that advocated by Tukey (1977) for exploratory data analysis.[1] He noted that graphic displays strengthen comparisons of the data by permitting researchers to see how the data behave generally as well as how points deviate from the general

---

[1] We also employed a software program, Data Desk, that was developed from Tukey's work. Some of the graphs appear in Chaps. V and VI.

pattern. Tukey claimed that exploratory data analysis is like detective work, with graphs forcing the researcher to notice the unexpected.

The approach also corresponds with ethnographic qualitative data analysis (Goetz & LeCompte, 1984; Miles & Huberman, 1984). Miles and Huberman noted that displaying data in a systematic fashion is essential to sorting and condensing information to the conceptual core in order to make general statements about ethnographic or qualitative data. They advocated abstracting data from the idiosyncratic details of a case and argued for the use of numbers when appropriate to characterize the textual data and for checking back to the raw data in order to be sure that generalized statements are grounded in the individual cases.

A number of other researchers have developed related ways of systematizing ethnographic or qualitative data (Cazden et al., 1979; Green & Wallat, 1979; Mehan, 1979; Mehan & Riel, in press; Moore, 1981). Systematic analyses of functional patterns in interactional data also appear in other scholarly traditions, such as ethology (Grossmann, 1981), infant social interaction research (Als, Tronick, & Brazelton, 1979; Uzgiris & Fafouti-Milenkovic, 1985), and the hermeneutic tradition (Kreppner, Paulsen, & Schuetze, 1982).

Our analysis was a process of abstraction from contextually rich ethnographic analyses of the data from each family to a systematic examination of the generality and variations in patterns appearing in the 14 families from each of the four cultural communities. The coding categories were derived in a process of abstraction from the ethnographic descriptions, progressively developing a common language that we believed fairly represented the gist of the events. The common language for looking at patterns across the four communities was arrived at through a dialogue among the researchers representing these communities, in which we discussed and revised the common language of analysis until it satisfied us as both capturing the important variations and fairly representing the practices of the families in each community. The abstracted, reduced data did not maintain the rich idiosyncratic context of each family; rather, it attempted to develop an abstracted language for use across cases that reflected the focal variations in the families' approaches.

This process resembles Berry's (1969) recommendation for derived etic research, in which researchers approach a project with preconceived ideas (*imposed etic*), then study how the issues take form for natives of the community (*emic*), and finally synthesize the emic with the original imposed etic perspective to derive a general approach that is more faithful to the local meanings of the people observed (*derived etic*).

The analysis of the observations in the current study thus followed four main steps, which are described in the remainder of this chapter:

33

1. An ethnographic description of the record for each family in each community;
2. The development of a common language with which to describe similarities and differences occurring across families and communities;
3. The coding of the record of each family according to this system; and
4. The graphic and statistical analysis of the coded data and the condensing of results into a communicative form for readers.

METHODS USED TO DESCRIBE EACH CASE

The 1½–2-hour videotapes were first described ethnographically, focusing on the meaning of the actions and the speech of the child and the caregivers in the specific activity. A common set of guidelines was used for the descriptions in the four cultural settings so that a similar approach and level of detail would be employed. The similarity in the four researchers' approaches to description was checked by cross-describing numerous segments of observations from the United States, with which all four were familiar. By the time we began writing the "official" descriptions, the differences among them seemed minor and not to reflect differences in interpretation. Although length varied, for the most part the same material appeared in the overlapping descriptions of the same observation, as can be seen in the following descriptions made by each of the four investigators, involving a 12-month-old Salt Lake boy, his mother, and the embroidery hoop (a metal ring with handles that release it from inside a plastic ring when they are squeezed together; see Fig. 1 above).

Transcript 1
Mother holds the hoop up toward Stanley [a pseudonym] and starts to manipulate it.
Stanley becomes interested. He watches what his mother does and reaches for the hoop with a lusty "Hah! Haaah!"
The view is obscured for a moment, during which the mother probably released the inner ring very briefly and returned it, without vocalization.
Stanley grasps the hoop.
The mother smiles, lets him have it, and sits back.
She looks up at the baby with a smile and asks, "What *is* that?"
The baby looks through the hole of the hoop.
The mother reaches for the handles, saying, "Look. . . . Look at this."

The baby doesn't stop in his activity, which is to bring the hoop to his face and peek through the hole.

The mother and others laugh at his insistence, and the mother continues trying to get hold of the handles.

The baby turns away from her and pulls the hoop away, bringing it up to the top of his head.

The mother laughs, "Oh, you're going to put it on your head, huh?"

Transcript 2

The mother just slightly separates the two rings in front of the baby's face.

"Huah!" the baby laughs. "Ha! Ha! Huuh!" Baby laughs and reaches up and grabs the rings as the mother slides the rings together again.

Mother laughs and lets go of the hoop as the baby takes it.

Baby examines the hoop interestedly.

Mother leans on her elbows toward baby at the coffee table. Smiling, she asks baby in a mildly enthusiastic tone, "What is that! . . . Look." She reaches out for the hoop as baby peers through the circle at her, framing his face. "Oh, hah!" mother laughs humorously.

Baby continues to clutch the hoop tightly and turns away from mother, sliding the hoop on his head like a halo.

Mother and everyone laugh. Mother continues to reach for the hoop, attempting to squeeze the handles, but hesitating from taking it from baby. "Oh, you're gonna put it on yer head, huh?" mother says in an amused tone.

Transcript 3

Stanley is interested. He looks at the hoops and then reaches for them. His mother lets him take the hoops, as she settles herself into a more comfortable position. She then reaches over to try to demonstrate how to take the hoops apart. She tries to do this while Stanley is busy mouthing the hoops. She tries to direct his attention to her action, saying, "What is this? Look at this."

Stanley now puts the hoops on his head.

The mother laughs and comments, "Oh, you want to put it on your head."

Transcript 4

The child mumbles and gets the hoop from the mother as she attempts to part the pieces. "What is that? Look, what is it?" asks the mother, again trying to part the pieces as the child holds the hoop. The child doesn't let this happen and puts the hoop on his head and turns away from the mother, who acknowledges the child's action by saying in acceptance, "Oh, you're putting it on your head, huh?"

That we four usually described events very similarly makes us confident that we were working successfully with similar criteria for interpretation. Independent descriptions by Pablo Chavajay (a native of San Pedro) of the San Pedro and Salt Lake data were also very similar.

The descriptions were used in conjunction with the videotaped records for all later coding, with the videotaped records having priority and the descriptions largely serving to keep track of the flow of events. Relying on the videotapes was indispensable, especially for capturing specific attention patterns and means of communication. The description process was also essential, however, in orienting us to the patterns that we wanted to capture in the subsequent coding scheme and in helping focus our later observation of the videotapes.

The central aim of the description was to portray the efforts of the participants in a way that was faithful to their situation and at the same time comprehensible to someone from another background. The descriptions were approached as an exercise in writing drama: we attempted to give sufficient interpretation and contextualization of the observation to enable an unfamiliar reader to visualize the scenario or to act out the sense and feeling of the event.

The descriptions were done by the investigators representing each community (Rogoff and Mosier each described all Mayan sessions; Rogoff and Mosier, with the help of Jamie Germond and Amy Urbanek, were the primary describers of the U.S. data; Mistry described all Indian sessions; and Göncü described all Turkish sessions). The investigators had been present at the sessions and thus were familiar with the family situation and the nature of the session. Before beginning the description of a session, they reminded themselves of family background information and sometimes made a catalog of the main events of the session, to help avoid the temptation to describe everything in detail. The next section reports the guidelines used for our ethnographic descriptions.

Guidelines for Description

Interpretation was essential in order to go beyond simply writing down behaviors out of context, which would render them meaningless. The guiding questions were the following: What is going on? What appears to be the reason that the child or caregiver did something? What is the overriding theme of a segment of the interaction (or of the whole interaction so far)?

The primary focus of description was the function of the participants' actions rather than the minutiae of behaviors; thus, the descriptions focused on the purpose of actions for communication or for accomplishing some other goal. For events that related to the questions addressed in this *Mono-*

graph, we indicated the evidence available in the participants' behavior that convinced the viewer of their purposes—for example, that a child appeared frustrated with an object and tried to elicit her mother's assistance by crying and waving the object in the air while looking at her mother. When uncertain, we included notes indicating that the interpretation was a guess. Just writing down the child's behaviors (crying, looking at the mother) would not have been adequate for a reader to determine what was "going on."

We attempted to be poetic and evocative in describing events, to allow a reader to visualize the scene and to understand not only the behaviors but also the feeling and tone of the event. We found it useful to expand the vocabulary that we were used to using in psychology and to include anything that would get the point across, including analogies to familiar situations. For example, if the mother and child were struggling over a toy and the child grudgingly gave it up to the mother with a resigned sigh, such a description gets the picture across better than saying that the mother reached for the toy that the child held, the child drew it toward herself quickly, the mother grasped the toy, the child did not let go, then the mother pulled on the toy again, and the child let go with a glance at the mother with furrowed brows, and so on. The behaviors are an important supplement to the description of the purposes, but they do not get the point across on their own.

Special attention was paid to the nonverbal aspects of the situation because we have found that many people (especially middle-class Caucasians with university training) find them more difficult to attend to than the verbal interaction. To understand an event, nonverbal actions such as changes in posture, eye contact, gaze aversion, and intonation are essential. For example, it is relevant whether a mother's invitation to "put the toy here" is accompanied with a finger tapping on the place to put the toy, whether the mother guides the child's movements with her arms, and whether her gaze provides further information. Again, the focus is on the meaning rather than the motions.

Although the events of most interest involved the caregivers and the child, the actions of other people were relevant as they affected such interaction or helped interpret it. For example, the fact that the interviewer was asking questions was indicated since it influenced the kind of attention the caregiver could give the child, but the content of the interviewer-mother conversation was usually irrelevant. It was important to attend especially to the interaction between the caregiver and the child at the times that the child was not the caregiver's main focus. For example, was the caregiver oblivious to the child, or was she subtly monitoring the child's activities while giving primary attention to the interviewer? Or did the caregiver give priority to the child over the interviewer, allowing or encouraging the child to interrupt the adult activity?

The absence of an action that might otherwise be expected provided very useful information. In order to note down what the mother did *not* do, it was helpful to keep in mind how other mothers handled similar situations. Focusing on the purpose of the mother's actions facilitated attention to the absence as well as the presence of certain actions. For example, it allowed interpretations such as "The mother is engaged in answering the interviewer's questions and does not interrupt this activity to attend to the child even when the child holds objects up in her line of vision or when the child fiddles with the interviewers' belongings."

The transcript began with a description of the setting in sufficient detail for a reader to visualize the scenario and the position of the cast of characters, including onlookers and other people present. It included a rough map of the household layout indicating the positions of the participants during the observation. Events were marked according to the footage of the incident, to aid in finding the incident again. Descriptions indicated transitions from one activity to another to indicate what brought on an activity (e.g., did the researcher suggest that the mother give the child a snack, or did the mother spontaneously bring out crackers?). Any instructions given to the caregiver were included as well as the toddler's attention to such instructions, especially when the novel objects were brought out.

Sometimes the transcript was segmented into turns taken by the child and the caregivers. However, some interchanges were better communicated without breaking them apart according to child and caregiver. For example, it was more useful to note "the child hands the mother the toy" than to have to break it into "the child offers the toy to the mother" and "the mother receives the toy."

Much of the footage could be summarized briefly simply to provide the context of what occurred between major incidents. Without such summarizing, ethnographic description would take forever, and analysis would be stymied by too much peripheral information. Unimportant detail could be avoided by noting the general direction of events, stating, for example, "While the mother answers questions and monitors the child, the child plays near her feet with his own toys and occasionally glances up at her, holding up a toy and vocalizing." Even with these guidelines, description of the 1½ hours of data took on average 30 hours and 30 typed, single-spaced pages.

DEVELOPING A COMMON LANGUAGE FOR ANALYSES ACROSS FAMILIES AND COMMUNITIES

As the descriptions for each family were nearing completion, the four investigators conferred to develop a common language—a system of classifications—for abstraction of the information. We extended our initial notions of cultural similarities and differences in guided participation to the circumstances observed in each community in order to develop an overall classification scheme that focused more closely on the question of whether children took responsibility for learning with adult support or adults took responsibility for organizing children's learning. This stage of our analysis also involved deciding how to segment the observations to allow for coding comparable units of observation across the different families and communities.

This process entailed extensive dialogue to refine categories in order to capture important nuances and avoid inappropriate value judgments in any community. Each of us had to teach the others to understand the phenomena from the perspective of the community that each represented. For example, we began by contrasting verbal and nonverbal means of communication but felt that "nonverbal" was insufficiently precise for the means that were used in San Pedro and Dhol-Ki-Patti; we eventually ended up distinguishing between nonverbal means involving adjustment of objects or of the partner's hands, gestures, and intense gaze, touch, posture, and timing cues.

CODING OF OBSERVATIONS

This section describes how we selected segments of the stream of events for analysis (novel objects, dressing, and novel object exploration during adult activity), the specific variables that we ended up analyzing and their definitions, and their reliabilities. Figure 2 presents an overview of the variables that were analyzed for this report.[2] The variables are presented and defined in this chapter in the order in which they were introduced in the discussion of cultural universals and variations in the introduction (this order is maintained throughout the *Monograph*). Unless otherwise indicated, the variables were coded in terms of whether they ever occurred in a given episode.

Segmentation: Identifying Activity Episodes

The segmentation of the data involved identifying similar activity episodes across each family's interview: up to five episodes involving novel objects, one episode involving dressing, and one episode involving novel object exploration during adult activity (if there was one). The five novel objects were chosen from the total number presented on the basis of

[2] We do not report a number of other variables that were later dropped owing to overlap with variables that were kept, lack of conceptual clarity, or low reliability.

Coding of Observations

Number of **interactional moves** by child: 1-3 4-9 10-20 21+
Resp. partners_____ Adult?_____Child? age_____

Caregivers' agenda _____
Child's agenda_____

Mutual involvement of caregivers and child?____

Child **introduces** info/structure?____   Child **seeks greater involvement?** _____

Talk to child: 10+sntnc   4-9sntnc   1-3sntnc   1-3phrases   Words   None
Child Talk: 4+phrases   1-3phrases   4+words   1-3words   None

Caregiver introduces/**orients** nature of activity: Verbally   Nonverbally   Neither
Caregiver **simplifies**: Verbal Adjust obj./hands Gesture Gaze/Touch/Posture/Timing
Child **seeks greater assistance**:   Verbal   Gesture   Gaze/Touch/Posture/Timing
Child **seeks clarification** through gaze?____

Caregivers' explanation: **extending** to other situations? _____

Caregivers' **demonstration**	Extensive	Moderate	Brief	None
before child participates	____	____	____	____
during child participation	____	____	____	____

Caregiver **directs attention** to process? ____   **Turns task over** to child? ____

Caregiver acts as **playmate?**____
Ad. caregiver treats child as **conversational peer**____   Ch. takes conv. peer role____

Caregiver used marked **babytalk** intonation? ____
Caregiver **vocab. lesson:** Labels Commentary Expands Requests label   Lang. games
Child **vocab. lesson:**   Labels   Requests label   Lang. games

Mock excitement to motivate child's involvement?_____
Caregiver **praise/cheer**_____

Caregiver mostly **poised ready to help?** _____

Child clearly **refuses/insists?**____   Caregiver **overrules child's** demand?____

Attention management in presence of competing events
Attn. was: Simultaneous   Alternating   Unaware

CHILD	(__)_____	(__)_____	(__)_____
CAREGIVERs	(__)_____	(__)_____	(__)_____

Interruption of adult activity for child purposes____

Engagement **embedded in group?** _____

Fig. 2.—Coding sheet for observations, indicating the format of coding for the variables that were retained through the analysis. (Dropped variables have been deleted.)

having aroused the most reliable interest in all four communities. We also considered analyzing other types of episodes—feeding, social play, and play with the children's own objects. However, differences in procedure across communities made these episodes difficult to compare, and our informal examination of these other episodes suggested that they did not challenge the conclusions to be drawn from the episodes that we did select.

The regular novel objects episodes were child focused, with the caregiver having been given or taking responsibility for helping the child. The caregiver focused attention on the activity of the child and did not supersede this focus with attention to adult-adult interaction independent of the child's activity. In novel object exploration during adult activity, caregivers were involved in adult conversation or other activities but gave some attention to the child.

The reason for including analysis of novel object exploration during adult activity was our impression that some of the children, especially in San Pedro and Dhol-Ki-Patti, were uncomfortable with being the focus of adult attention and became more involved in exploring the novel objects with their caregiver when adults were engaged with each other. Our analyses focus primarily on the child-focused novel objects episodes because we usually had five episodes of this type per family but only one episode for dressing and a highly variable number of episodes of novel object exploration during adult activity. We employed the episodes of dressing and novel object exploration during adult activity to examine the extent to which our novel objects observations resembled guided participation during other types of activity.

The unit of analysis was each episode in which the child was engaged with a caregiver with a specific novel object or in dressing. An episode included four or more interactional moves by the child (either initiated by the child or responsive) toward any responsible partner (excluding the interviewers) and at least one move by the caregiver.[3] There needed to be joint engagement at some point between the child and a caregiver, but there could at times be moves made by one to which the other did not respond, as long as there was at least one move by the caregiver. An episode could involve brief interruptions from intervening activity, such as short periods of adult-oriented conversation during child-oriented novel object episodes, and could stop and start up again later.

[3] In San Pedro and Keçiören, all five novel objects elicited at least this amount of interaction. For two Salt Lake children, one novel object elicited less than this amount of interaction; interactions involving a similar novel object were substituted. In Dhol-Ki-Patti, two of the novel objects routinely did not elicit interest and were dropped, and interactions involving another novel object were also occasionally substituted for one or another of the remaining novel objects when little interaction occurred.

Our analyses included only activities in which the toddler was involved with caregivers—that is, adults or responsible children who direct or supervise the toddler in the episode in question. If the child had several responsible partners, we coded their interactions together (summing across individuals) rather than differentiating each caregiver.

As an aid in identifying episodes, we began by indicating the nature of the partner's and child's agendas in narrative as a way of orienting to the primary purposes that the episode had for the participants before dealing with individual variables. Examples of partners' agendas include getting the child to work an object, keeping the child from interrupting adult conversation, and keeping peace between siblings. Examples of children's agendas include getting access to an object, working a toy, and getting the caregiver's attention.

Novel object exploration during adult activity.—Episodes could be initiated by either the child or the caregiver. For an episode to count as novel object exploration during adult activity, the adult caregiver did not have to be very actively involved in the adult conversation but must at least have been attending to it and following it (e.g., laughing along with jokes, glancing around at appropriate times, inserting appropriate comments). The adult could attend to the child during junctures in adult conversation (e.g., when the interviewer was looking for the next question), but it had to be clear that the caregiver remained in readiness to continue the adult conversation/ activity rather than being willing to drop the adult focus. This could be indicated by maintaining a postural openness to the adult activity or by glances to check when she was being addressed. Examples would include a caregiver casually demonstrating an object to the child during adult conversation or responding to a child's whining with a few moves to solve the problem and then returning to adult conversation without extending the interaction with the child.

We included instances during which the caregiver handled the interaction by giving her attention alternately to the child and the adult activity as well as those during which she gave her attention to both simultaneously. The adult could attend heavily to the child during the episode, but not lose track of the adult activity for long stretches; interruptions to attend to the child could not exceed two or three child-focused moves.

We counted the number of episodes of novel object exploration during adult activity in each community and analyzed the one with the longest and most coherent series of moves, giving priority to novel objects that we had coded for child-focused novel objects episodes. The agenda had to be consistent with a use of the object that we would include in regular novel objects episodes—working it, not just handling it or using it to get the child to quit doing something.

Dressing episodes.—Dressing episodes focused on one round of putting on and taking off an item with sleeves (or, if such an item was not available, one that required putting limbs through other holes). For comparability, priority was given to elicited dressing events over spontaneous ones. Other agendas within a dressing episode (e.g., a game that develops) could be coded, and there could be intervening events before completion of the episode, just as with novel objects.

Definitions of Variables: Universal Processes of Guided Participation

Creating Bridges between Caregiver and Child Understanding

Mutual involvement was coded if both the child and the caregivers attended to each other's moves and provided direction to the activity, by agreeing, initiating, and making at least some elaborations on each other's moves, although not necessarily to an equal extent. One partner could make suggestions and the other follow through, but the latter must also make moves to which the partner responded. The partners did not have to be involved with the same agenda, but the agendas had to fit together.

Caregiver orients child involved introducing new information or structure to the child (at any point in the episode) regarding the overall goals or a key part of the event or what was expected in the situation. Orienting framed a major goal, not just specific little directives for particular actions. The extent of verbal as opposed to nonverbal orienting was analyzed for variation across communities. To count as telling the child what to do, words had to carry information regarding the general agenda, not just a direction to "do it," although they did not need to be complete in themselves (e.g., "Pull it like this" while pulling the jumping-jack string would be coded as both verbal and nonverbal). Sometimes the orienting did not explain what to do but told the child in other ways what kind of activity it was, such as introducing the jar by saying, "What's inside there?" and peering closely into the jar.

Structuring

Caregiver simplifies involved attempts to facilitate the child's efforts by handling part of the task (e.g., holding the jumping jack high to facilitate the child's grasp of the bottom ball), dividing the task into subtasks (e.g., holding the bottom part of the jar while the child worked the lid), or handling complicated moves (e.g., fitting the lid of the pencil box on so that the child could slide it in).

Child introduces information or structure involved ideas volunteered or developed by the child that built or redirected the *joint* activity.

43

Child seeks clarification included whether children ever attempted to access the caregivers' interpretation of an ambiguous situation using visual social referencing, that is, turning questioningly toward the caregiver to "ask" what to do or how to interpret a situation.

Child seeks involvement involved the child spontaneously trying to take over all or part of the task, with greater involvement than the moment before (indicating "I wanna do it myself").

Child seeks assistance involved the child seeking more help with the task than the child was currently receiving; it is more than expressing frustration *at* the object.

Definitions of Variables: Cultural Variations in Guided Participation

Verbal and Nonverbal Communication

Talk to child was broken down into units of 10 or more sentences, four to nine sentences, one to three sentences, one to three phrases, solitary words, or no words. *Child's talk* was broken down into units of four or more phrases, one to three phrases, four or more words, one to three words, or no words. We coded the total amount of talk to the child by all responsible partners and the highest level of child talk. Sentences contained four or more words but did not need to be grammatically complete; shorter phrases (two or three words) and words were given partial credit. Children's phrases were combinations of words that were beyond holophrases (e.g., not "thank you" but "the boat" or "dat mine") and that contained words that the child could move around. Child talk counted repetitions of the same words or phrases.

Caregiver orients child, caregiver simplifies, and *child seeks assistance* involved the variables described under cultural universals, distinguished in terms of whether the communication occurred verbally or through adjustment of the object or the partner's hands, gestures, or gaze, touch, posture, or timing. We coded only means that specifically added information or guidance, not those just accompanying some other form of communication that carried all the information. For each of these three variables, each episode was coded in terms of whether the means of communication was verbal, through adjustment of objects and partner's hands, gestural, or through gaze, touch, posture, or timing cues:

> Verbal means included words and stylized vocalizations that carried specific information, including sound effects like "bing" to show the springing of the ring's handles or making conventional animal sounds.

Adjustment of objects and partner's hands included direct joint action that facilitated communication or efforts in a way that appeared central or intended for communication. Putting hands over the child's to help work an object counted as adjustment; distal demonstrations did not.

Gestural means included symbolic action, not direct action, that could be understood by common knowledge or in context as standing for an idea. Gestures could be conventional actions with widely understood local meaning (such as nods, shrugs, bye-bye waves, peek-a-boo gestures, palm-up object requests, and points) or nonconventional but stylized gestures such as suggesting to open something with a twisting motion in the air. Gestures included offers and requests that were smoothly accomplished but excluded simply acting directly on the object (e.g., grabbing something away or reaching directly for an object), and they omitted the first offer of an object to the child at the beginning of an activity.

Gaze, touch, posture, and timing cues included intent gaze and touch, posture, or timing cues that carried communicative force and did not have an equally convincing noncommunicative explanation. Gaze involved intent eye contact or visual expressions (e.g., raised brows) that were not conventional gestures, such as a questioning glance, a stern gaze, pointing with the eyes at an event to be noticed, underlining a point with intensity of gaze, winking, or sticking one's face in the other's face so as to be able to communicate with the eyes. Just glancing, making eye contact, or monitoring that did not seem to have a message in itself or that was a necessary part of a game did not count. Touch, posture, and timing cues included shifts in touching the other person, posture, and timing changes, such as nudging the child's elbow to indicate when to do something, moving an object with exaggerated motion to draw attention to critical features of a process, or meaningful added intensity or suspenseful timing of gestures (e.g., an especially firm and marked offer of the jumping-jack string, highlighting the directive to "use it" with force and clarity of motion).

Child seeks clarification, described under universals in guided participation, was also analyzed to examine cultural variation in this form of nonverbal communication (visual social referencing).

Explanation and Demonstration

Caregiver extending to other situations explained a situation by referring to another context in a meaningful way that was not explicitly called for by the usual name or use of the object. This included making analogies ("This is like your nesting boxes"), referring to an object or an event with a label that put the whole thing into a certain frame of action (e.g., pointing out that the jumping jack was "dancing"), or acting out a familiar scenario to clarify the event (e.g., saying "Peekaboo" when the puppet popped out or moving the child's legs in imitation of the jumping jack's).

Caregiver's demonstration before and during child participation (coded as extensive, moderate, brief, or none) could include either joint action with the caregiver mainly responsible or symbolic demonstrations to the child (e.g., indicating the action without the object). "Before participation" meant before the toddler started working the object even in a rudimentary way. "Extensive" demonstration involved many demonstrations or several complex ones, to the extent that it was difficult to imagine anything else the caregiver could do to demonstrate (compared with the range exhibited before or during child participation in that activity across the four communities); "moderate" demonstration involved situations in which several good demonstrations were given but one could imagine more or more elaborate ones; "brief" demonstration was abbreviated or cursory or involved few instances. For dressing, there had to be an instructional aspect to the activity (e.g., showing the child how to free his or her hand to get it in a sleeve by demonstrating how to transfer an object to the other hand), or the caregiver could provide assistance to a child who was managing the activity.

Caregiver directs attention to process provided a general marker indicating that the child should pay attention to some (otherwise unspecified) process of an ongoing event, by saying "Look," "Watch," or "See?" or using cues that tell the child no more than "Look now," such as by moving an object right in front of the child's face. This category excluded efforts that were simply attempts to recruit the child's interest and involvement in the activity.

Turns task over to child meant spontaneously handing over the whole task to the child or urging a hesitant child to try, indicating "You're ready to do this now," after the task was offered to the child for the first time.

Adult-Child Roles in Teaching and Learning

Caregiver acts as playmate involved entering into equal status through mutual involvement in play, not just being excited, using a playful voice, or directing the child to play. The caregiver needed to take on a peer role verbally or in actions, entering into games such as tickle and chase, pretend role play, or peek-a-boo as a partner in play.

Adult converses with child as peer and *child converses with adult as peer* attempted to capture whether the child was ever treated or ever acted as a person of equal status with valuable opinions and ideas rather than as a subordinate who may receive directives, request clarification, or indicate understanding but not initiate or direct conversation. Caregiver-child peer conversation involved the child in reciprocal verbal dialogue in conditions other than those necessary for the action under way. The caregiver's role had to include talk; the child's could include talk, protowords, or nods.

The adult could invite the child to participate in conversation or participate in the child's initiations (e.g., asking the child's opinion, asking the child a question with a known answer in order to encourage conversation, pausing in a series of small-talk questions to encourage the child to take conversational turns, or responding to the child's comments or vocalizations as if they were conversational turns). It was not considered peer conversation if the caregiver simply suggested an action by asking, "Do you want to do this yourself?" and the child simply took the object. The adult's move needed to call for or expect a vocal or symbolic response (e.g., if the caregiver asked the child's opinion of something—"Is it pretty?"—and paused for a conversational response from the child).

The child could initiate peer conversation (e.g., offering small talk or opinions, interrupting adult conversation for child comments, asking questions that were not necessary for carrying out an activity that an adult had suggested or approved) or direct the action verbally in ways that were not simply responsive to adults' directives (i.e., going beyond simply clarifying what an adult just asked the child to do). Unobtrusively expressing interest in something or vocalizing to get an adult's attention was not coded as taking a peer role.

Caregiver uses babytalk intonation involved any modification of pitch or intonation or specialized vocabulary not acceptable for use with local adults. Simplified, short sentences and pet names were not by themselves babytalk.

Caregiver vocabulary lesson (labels, commentary, expands, requests label, language games) and *child vocabulary lesson* (labels, requests label, language games) focused on teaching language beyond simply ensuring communication. They called attention to features of language, teaching the meanings of words and testing the child's knowledge, deliberately or not. The score for each episode ranged from 0 to 5 for *caregiver vocabulary lesson* and from 0 to 3 for *child vocabulary lesson*, depending on how many of the following categories were exhibited at all during the episode:

> "Labels objects or events" focused on teaching labels of objects (e.g., "That's his *eyes*" or "Boat!") or events ("See, the baby's *sitting*"). Labeling did not simply explain an action or announce an event; it focused on teaching vocabulary. Labeling by the toddler could be a response to a request, but not just parroting a caregiver's label.
> "Running commentary" was descriptive narration of events, apparently addressed to the toddler or to an invisible audience, with no obvi-

ous purpose besides providing a play-by-play account or an interpretation, much like a sports commentator. It included rhetorical questions not directly requesting information but providing interpretation (e.g., "You wanna put it in there?" after the toddler had already done so or had already made that intention clear).

"Expands or mimics child utterance" repeated the child's words or vocalizations or expanded them with improvement in pronunciation or wording (e.g., the child says, "Peh-ees," and the father echoes, "Pennies," or the child says, "Dat eyes," and the mother expands, "That's the eyes").

"Requests label" included the caregiver's requests for labels already known to the caregiver, in the form of test questions, or the child's requests for labels.

"Language games" involved word games (e.g., "What does a doggie say?") or games that tested verbal comprehension with questions that had obvious answers (e.g., "Is that the *eyes*?" or "Did you kiss the baby?" just after the child kissed the doll) if the adult waited for or requested an affirmation. The toddler was coded for provision of the requested communication.

Mock excitement invited or motivated the child to participate in an activity by means of exaggerated expressions of interest to try to engage or persuade the child. It was not real excitement or enthusiasm but pretend excitement to get the child's attention or to motivate the child.

Caregiver praise motivated the child through applause, congratulations, and other signs of praise for the child's achievement or for personal qualities such as cuteness. It focused on the child, not the event, conveying "how smart" or "how cute," either implicitly or explicitly. It was not simply feedback such as a flat "There you go" to mark completion of a task.

Caregiver poised ready to help indicated responsiveness to children's leadership in the activities. It was coded when the caregiver generally (not just occasionally) was alert and in a posture of readiness to assist the child, with body or hands held ready to aid the child at times other than when the caregiver was assisting the child. Evidence included holding the hands "in gear" or at attention rather than lax, small motions of the hands in anticipation of the child needing help or support, supporting an object in readiness to help the child, sitting in a posture of readiness to assist responsively, or reacting instantly when the child subtly indicated a need for help.

Caregiver overrules child was coded if the child refused or insisted and if the caregiver ever insisted on some aspect of the agenda (whether the caregiver's effort was successful or not). The child had to evidence clear refusal (not just lack of attention) or clear insistence (going beyond polite persistence). Caregiver insistence or refusal involved superseding the child's will, not just coaxing. Any tug of war indicated that both partners insisted.

Learning through Observation

Coding attention to competing events involved first deciding whether there was an event competing with the child's or the caregiver's focus of attention and then deciding whether the person in question attended to both events simultaneously, alternated rapidly between them, or seemed unaware of the competing event.

"Competing events" involved any extraneous event that was not part of the person's ongoing focus of attention. For the caregiver, only events in which the main or secondary focus involved the target child were coded. Competing events included bids for the person's attention away from the focus at hand, unrelated ongoing events that an alert person might monitor, or spontaneous management of attention to competing foci. Examples of competing events included such social events as another child bidding for a mother's attention, a phone call, a passerby or traveling salesperson calling out, or ongoing conversation external to the child's or caregiver's main focus as well as such nonsocial events as something falling or an unexpected airplane overhead. They were events that one might expect the person to monitor or to acknowledge, not just ongoing events that it would be strange for a person to attend or reply to (e.g., routine events in this setting or events that one should try to ignore).

Competing events needed to be extraneous to the main focus. If a person was putting aside an object to facilitate the main event, this was considered part of the main event. Onlookers chiming in with comments or laughter in ways that fit with what the child and caregiver were already doing, as echoes, would not be competing events; extraneous laughter or comments from an onlooker would be. Several people collaborating in the *same* activity (e.g., all helping the child with a toy at once) would not involve competing events unless they offered the child or the caregiver differing foci of attention at the same time. For example, a situation in which a mother needed to manage an older child who was interested in grabbing the novel object from the toddler would involve a competing event if the mother had to attend to two agendas at once or implement two strategies at once.

The attention management pattern was coded whenever there was a competing event, by first jotting down a shorthand description of the event under its category (attending to two events simultaneously, attending to two events alternately, or appearing unaware of a competing event) and, after the episode ended, judging the prevalence of each attentional category. The judgment of prevalence was used in order to control for differences among the communities and families in the number of competing events.[4] We used

[4] The few episodes that contained *no* competing events were eliminated from coding. They represented a very small proportion of the total episodes in all four communities:

the following scale to indicate what attentional category best characterized each episode:

4 = overwhelmingly prevalent, with very strong or frequent instances (but there could be an example or two of other categories);

3 = primary pattern of attention, more than any other category but not overwhelming;

2 = tied for first place with some other category (or both others);

1 = some of the category, but not as much as some other category; and

0 = none.

We took into account how long or often a particular category of attention occurred relative to the others as well as how effortful or compelling it was.

Attending to several events simultaneously involved active, uninterrupted attention to several activities. It did not necessarily involve simultaneous action, but simultaneous *attention,* which could be indicated by a reply to a competing event, by carrying out what was suggested, or by brief monitoring (e.g., the mother conversed with the interviewer at the same time as she assisted the child with an object; the child worked an object with the mother while interacting with another child; the mother used peripheral attention or sweeping eye movements like an air traffic controller to update several sources of information continually without seeming to lose track of any of them). It required evidence that two events were actively managed at once, with monitoring, directing, or responding to several sources simultaneously, not just placing one activity on hold while attending to the other event. It involved skilled action requiring continued attention or skillful participation, not automatic action or pliantly being acted on (e.g., just holding or fiddling with an object in a nonchallenging way, such as absently flipping the jumping jack or submitting to being dressed). In simultaneous attending, each activity would be uninterrupted by the other, with each line of attention maintained as smoothly as if there were no other focus. An example was provided by a San Pedro 20-month-old who repeatedly kept track of two or three competing events through the jar episode:

María watched her mother present the jar to explore while María simultaneously handed another toy over to her cousin; she monitored her mother demonstrating the jumping jack while she extracted the peewee doll from the jar; she noticed everything the interviewers did without breaking her activity with the jar; she monitored her cousin subtly tak-

---

zero in San Pedro; three episodes for children and three for caregivers in Salt Lake; two for caregivers in Dhol-Ki-Patti; and six for caregivers in Keçiören.

ing various objects while she admired the peewee doll and skillfully put it in the jar; and on and on.

Attending to several events alternately meant that, while attending to one focus, the person appeared interrupted or momentarily oblivious to others, alternating back and forth between the two (not just shifting away from the original focus without returning, which would not be coded at all). Alternating involved registering what was going on, noticing competing events, being alert to several foci of activity so that both activities were kept going, but nothing *demanding* being done in the secondary activity while attention was directed toward the primary activity; the secondary activity was put on hold. For example, a mother might stop mid-sentence in an adult conversation to answer a child's request and then return to the adult conversation.

Unaware was coded if the person appeared to be unaware of a competing event that one would expect a person to monitor or to which one would expect him or her to respond. It was coded only if there was something attention grabbing or unusual about the event to which a person would be expected to attend. If the person could be trying *not* to pay attention to an event (e.g., suppressing attention to a passing truck or a sibling interruption) or was not giving frequent evidence of attending to an ongoing, lengthy background activity, then the competing event was not coded since the attention management pattern was ambiguous.

Interruption of adult activity for child purposes involved the child obtrusively attempting to interrupt adult activity for the child's own purposes. The child could use intrusive vocalization or insistent tapping on an adult to attempt to break in or force the adult to look in a particular direction (by grabbing the adult's chin or sticking his or her face in the adult's face). Interruption did not include times that the child was simply being persistent in a polite request or trying to let an adult know something for the adult's purposes.

Engagement embedded in group meant that the toddler's involvement encompassed the overall complex, extradyadic engagements of a group. The code indicates the child's involvement with several people in complex shared activity; it is not an index of whether a group was present (a group was always present in our visits, including a caregiver, a child, two visitors, and often other kin or neighbors). We excluded dyadic focus in which the toddler's engagement was with one other person or several people successively, in what amounts to alternating dyadic focus. Being embedded in a group necessarily involved some common agenda, not just several people fighting over the same toy. Being an audience to an event involving several people was seldom a case of being embedded in a group, although an involved, observing child could be embedded in a group if there was a feel that the child was moving with the group. *Engagement embedded in group* was meant to capture the kind of coherent involvement in which more than two people may be involved—a kind of complex dance. In order to reach adequate reliability, we limited ourselves to coding substantial instances that were sustained or would serve as good examples of this category.

An example of being embedded in group activity was provided in the excerpt involving María given above. María *could* have interacted successively with her mother and then with her cousin, in what would have amounted to interactions with multiple dyads—instead, she appeared embedded in a group event. She smoothly coordinated her monitoring and protective efforts toward her encroaching cousin with her engagement with her mother regarding the novel objects. Her involvements in this episode could not have been disentangled into successive dyadic involvements but appeared rather to be a complex, multiway intertwining with the participants in the whole event.

Reliability of Coding

For the data from San Pedro and Salt Lake, reliability estimates were calculated between the two authors who were familiar with both communities for 100% of the San Pedro episodes and 61% of the Salt Lake episodes. Since we did not have second coders available for examining the reliability of coding for the Dhol-Ki-Patti and Keçiören data, we employed systematic cross-coded reliabilities on the Salt Lake data by the authors coding the Dhol-Ki-Patti and Keçiören data as proxy reliability estimates for those two communities. After achieving initial agreement between the four investigators on the Salt Lake data, we continued to code and discuss agreement on the Salt Lake data on a weekly basis in order to ensure against drift in coding definitions while the data for the other three communities were coded. With this extensive discussion throughout coding and our impression that there was very little drift, we feel confident that this proxy reliability strategy effectively represents the reliability with which the Dhol-Ki-Patti and Keçiören data were coded. The only difficulties resulting from this strategy occurred with a few variables (described below) that were very infrequent in the Salt Lake data, making assessment of proxy reliability impossible. The proxy codings used for estimating reliability are based on 61% of the Salt Lake episodes for Dhol-Ki-Patti and 63% of the Salt Lake episodes for Keçiören.

Reliability estimates were calculated for each individual episode, including novel objects, dressing, and novel object exploration during adult activity. This is more conservative than necessary for the novel objects data, as the results deal with averages across the novel objects. However, focusing on individual episodes occurs during our discussion of dressing and novel object exploration during adult activity. The only critical variables that were insufficiently reliable at the individual episode level were some of those involved in attention management. Hence, for these variables only, we calculated reliability estimates for novel objects on the average values rather than the individual episodes. In the one instance that was not sufficiently reliable at the individual episode level (the Keçiören proxy reliability for attending simultaneously), we do not discuss results obtained on this variable for dressing and novel object exploration during adult activity.

The estimates of reliability for the interval or scale variables were calculated using Pearson correlations, with a cutoff of .80 for an acceptable level of agreement. The r values ranged from .82 to 1.0, with a median r value of .96, for all such variables: talk to child, child's talk, caregivers' demonstration before child participates, caregivers' demonstration during child participation, caregiver vocabulary lesson, child vocabulary lesson, attending to several events simultaneously, attending to several events alternately, and unaware.

Reliabilities for categorical variables were calculated using kappa, for which .60 is an acceptable value (Gelfand & Hartmann, 1975). The κ values varied from .60 to 1.0, with a median of .86 for all the remaining variables listed in Figure 2 above, with the following exceptions. Six Dhol-Ki-Patti and Keçiören values were too low for inclusion in analyses (sometimes because rarity of occurrence in the Salt Lake data made estimation of proxy reliabilities difficult): mutual involvement in Dhol-Ki-Patti; child introduces information or structure in Keçiören; child seeks clarification in Dhol-Ki-Patti and Keçiören; caregiver overrules child in Dhol-Ki-Patti; and interruption of adult activity for child purposes in Keçiören. In addition, there were three values in Keçiören that were low but judged worth keeping because the disagreements were in a direction that would not jeopardize interpretation of the findings: caregiver uses babytalk intonation and caregiver overrules child (κ's = .58 and .49, with Göncü's codings systematically more conservative, assuring that the findings in Keçiören of a great extent of babytalk and of caregiver overruling are conservative results) and caregiver poised ready to help (κ = .59, with no systematic bias apparent and results clear-cut).

Further evidence of reliability can be derived from the similarity of our own conclusions to those drawn by Pablo Chavajay in his independent analyses of a portion of the San Pedro and Salt Lake data, which are included as an afterword to this *Monograph*. Chavajay, a native of San Pedro with an advanced degree from the University of San Carlos, had just arrived in the United States and spoke little English. He wrote his conclusions on the basis of independent viewing and description of four of the families from San Pedro and four from Salt Lake before he was informed of our questions or conclusions. As an experiment, we had asked Chavajay to carry out the same description process as we had and to make comparisons of the families in the two communities; the only orientation that we provided was the information that we were interested in children's learning and care-giver-child communication. (We provided assistance in translating the Salt Lake families' words, as he did for us with the Mayan statements in San Pedro.) We expected the process to yield interesting systematic differences both at the level of description and at the level of conclusions, which we intended to use as a window on cultural variation in interpretation of these events. However, Chavajay's transcripts and conclusions were extremely similar to our own, foiling the idea of using them to elucidate cultural variation but adding greatly to our confidence in the reliability of our observations and our conclusions.

GRAPHIC AND STATISTICAL ANALYSIS AND COMMUNICATION OF PATTERNS

Using the common language and classifications developed to handle the data analysis, the codings of each family were graphed in arrays like those presented in Chapters V and VI below, representing the distribution of all families' approaches within each community (median, central tendencies, range, and outliers) as well as the mean values. These arrays were used to check distributions within variables to be sure that we understood them as well as to examine patterns across variables. Inspection of patterns in the graphic arrays allowed us to consolidate or eliminate redundant variables and to abandon ambiguous variables.

Once we felt that we understood the pattern of community differences through examining the graphs, we checked our understanding further through statistical means (e.g., correlations and t tests) that also provide a reference criterion for communicating with readers about differences and similarities in patterns. The general understandings that we derived from the patterns in the graphs and the statistical analyses were checked and amplified through referring back to the videotapes and descriptions of both representative and anomalous families.

Our statistical analyses should be regarded merely as a tool supplementing the ethnographic and graphic analyses. They were not a means of discovery or confirmation—as were the descriptive and graphic analyses—but were simply used to check our conclusions and communicate them. They did allow us to drop some variables that were seen (through correlations) to be redundant or unreliable and to systematize our graphic analyses further. But they were not where we "found" our findings; the patterns that we describe derive from disciplined examination of data by informed people using statistics as just one of several tools.

Our statistical analyses of similarities and variations in guided participation focused on the episodes involving novel objects since we have five observations on each family for this activity, except in Dhol-Ki-Patti, where the number of novel object observations ranged from two to four per family (for reasons that we discuss in Chap. V). The analyses for novel objects are based on proportions averaged across the novel object observations. We considered the patterns observed in the two other kinds of episodes (dressing and novel object exploration during adult activity) in a more exploratory fashion because for each family there are at most one episode of dressing and one of novel object exploration during adult activity. However, examination of patterns in these situations allows an exploration of whether the patterns observed in guided participation across the two communities are limited to situations like the novel objects episodes, where caregivers were asked to help the children with objects, or whether the same patterns appear in other circumstances.

Although we considered several ways of lumping variables or communities together, we opted to use simple t tests for the main analyses rather than multivariate or four-community tests, even though there are a number of variables.[5] We did consider using Hotelling's t tests to perform multivariate tests, as some of our variables fall in clusters; however, we felt that the multivariate tests would obscure the results by lumping things together. Since the variables were conceptually motivated and distinguished, composites would not be of interest (for a similar approach, see Hoff-Ginsberg, 1991; for a discussion of situations in which multiple univariate analyses are called for rather than multivariate analyses, see Huberty & Morris, 1989). The different analyses that we performed are not assumed to be unrelated; rather, they provide the opportunity to examine converging evidence regarding the conceptual issues they represent, through examining each variable's role in the pattern rather than using composites.

We focus our analyses on variables that are conceptually motivated, with specific predictions and examination of how the variables together inform each other, and we use more conservative significance levels to interpret purely exploratory analyses (e.g., gender and age differences are not reported unless $p < .01$). In addition, our t tests employ separate estimates of variance, which is a conservative approach, because we do not want to assume that the population variances of our samples are equal. (This procedure reduces the degrees of freedom when the variances of the two samples are quite different, which is why the degrees of freedom differ from one t test to another.)

---

[5] ANOVAs were used to explore the possibility of toddlers' age and gender differences within communities; in the case of one variable in which toddlers' age had a strong relation to the finding, the results are presented in ANOVA form.

We decided against putting all four communities into one analysis of variance design because we wanted to be able to examine specific patterns of community differences for which we had predictions. Although applying planned comparisons was another alternative that we considered, we decided that our goal of examining patterns across variables within communities would not be well served if we put all the communities into one analysis for each variable. Planned comparisons across the four communities would focus on each variable rather than on the coherence of patterns among them in each community. In addition, t tests seemed more appropriate because the comparison of San Pedro and Salt Lake was for us logically and chronologically prior to the examination of the other two communities; although we expected Dhol-Ki-Patti to resemble San Pedro and Keçiören to resemble Salt Lake, we wanted to be more open to areas in which they did not follow the pattern of the San Pedro/Salt Lake contrast.

Hence, we first analyzed the differences between San Pedro and Salt Lake and treated the other two communities as follow-up analyses of the generality of the findings. The analyses for Dhol-Ki-Patti involve examination of similarities with San Pedro and differences with Salt Lake, with statistical tests focusing on the differences with Salt Lake and occasionally employed to compare Dhol-Ki-Patti with San Pedro if the pattern was discrepant. Similarly, the analyses for Keçiören involved examination of similarities with Salt Lake and differences with San Pedro, with statistical tests primarily used to test the differences with San Pedro and occasionally with Salt Lake. The next three chapters describe our findings, using parallel organization first to examine the patterns in San Pedro and Salt Lake and then to determine whether the patterns extend to another non-middle-class community, Dhol-Ki-Patti, and to another middle-class community, Keçiören.

In the chapters that follow, we present the data by means of narratives, graphs, and statistics that aid in describing the patterns and qualifying our statements. Readers who are familiar with psychological research are likely to find the statistics to be consistent with the kind used in the literature (although we opted for more descriptive than composite statistical approaches). What differs in our methods from those typically used in psychological research is the systematic testing of our ideas through ethnographic description and graphic techniques.

Although getting a "sense" of the data through piloting and examination of preliminary graphs is seen as desirable in psychological research, it is our impression that close analyses of the *meaning* of the events observed and of the *distribution of individual cases* are given insufficient systematic attention and are often overlooked. One of our purposes in this *Monograph* is to provide a model for those who are interested in making more systematic use of the meaning of events in individual cases and of systematic ways to classify and examine the distribution of cases to arrive at abstractions of patterns that fit the cases observed. For the process of coming to understand the patterns that we discuss in this *Monograph*, it was essential to examine the ideas through narrative case descriptions to arrive at classifications that did justice to the meanings available in each case and to examine the patterns of these classifications through graphic arrays of distributions. Our technique amounts to a combination of qualitative and quantitative approaches, using the analytic tools of various disciplines (anthropology and sociology in addition to psychology) to help discern the patterns and examine their coherence.[6]

The results chapters provide an indication of the narrative case descriptions through the use of illustrations of particular phenomena. The narrative descriptions in their complete form, however, are far more than illustrations—they cover the whole corpus of our observations of the visits to each family, before the information was segmented into episodes and classifications made of the phenomena that appeared central on the basis of the ethnographic analyses. These extensive ethnographic descriptions were the step in the analysis that yielded a segmentation and a classification that we regard as representing crucial features of the observations, true to the larger picture of these families and these communities. They were also used to make sense of the patterns and anomalies that appeared in the graphic and statistical analyses.

The graphic analyses that we employed are indicated in Chapters V and VI, where graphs are provided that show the distributions of families on key variables in order to relate the patterns observed in Dhol-Ki-Patti and Keçiören, respectively, to the patterns presented in Chapter IV for San Pedro and Salt Lake. The graphs presented in the *Monograph* are used to communicate the patterns to the readers; the original use of the graphs was much more extensive. They were a key tool in testing the patterns across variables and across communities in a way that represented the distribution of individual families in each community (through the use of medians, central tendencies, ranges, and outliers) as well as the average values for each community (the means).

Of course, a document like this *Monograph* does not present the details of every step in the analysis but rather summarizes what was learned from

---

[6] It has been our experience during the review process that this *Monograph* underwent that researchers find our approach to be rather conventional with regard to the analytic tool with which they are familiar (statistics, graphs, ethnography). That is a good sign, as it indicates that the tools are being used in ways that fit their usual practice; however, our hope is that readers can see past the use of the specific tool with which they are most familiar to consider how these tools can be combined in a systematic and scholarly way, advancing understanding in ways that move across the disciplines to achieve a broader view.

the steps along the way. However, we hope that the presentation of results helps the reader understand not only the pattern of findings but also the pattern-analysis process, which consisted of detective work to search for and abstract patterns to which individual cases contribute, using descriptive narratives, graphic arrays, and statistical analyses all as tools to search for converging evidence in a systematic manner.

IV. GUIDED PARTICIPATION IN SAN PEDRO
AND SALT LAKE

Barbara Rogoff and Christine Mosier

Before describing similarities and differences in our videotaped observations in San Pedro and Salt Lake, we describe the communities and provide background information on the 14 families in each community. Our descriptions are based on living in these two communities for years and on conversations during the interviews as well as on ethnographic work conducted in San Pedro (e.g., Rogoff, 1976); the information on the families comes from the interviews that we conducted during the visits with the families. In our background section, we focus especially on differences in age segregation of the children and on goals of development, both of which are important aspects of guided participation.

BACKGROUND OF THE COMMUNITIES AND THE FAMILIES

San Pedro

San Pedro is a Mayan Indian town in the highlands, on the shore of Lake Atitlán. It is a very compact town, with about 8,000 people living in the space of about 1 square km at the time of the visits we made for this study (1986).

Like the other communities, San Pedro is changing rapidly. In 1974, when Rogoff began working in San Pedro, the population was about 5,000, electricity was just being introduced to the town (although many families had battery-run radios), running water was seldom available in households (it was fetched from public faucets within a block or so), travel was by boats that arrived twice a week from across the lake or by periodic buses lumbering over the rocky road around the volcano on which San Pedro is perched, and schooling seldom extended beyond the third grade (25% of the children did not attend school at all).

By the time of our visits for the current study, some families had televisions, most had a tap somewhere in the extended family household, boats arrived on a daily basis, and the town had begun to produce a number of schoolteachers (for many of whom there was no employment). By 1991, some families received cable television or had videocassette recorders, the town had a public telephone, access to clean water was still a problem, travel across the lake had become a San Pedro enterprise with boats leaving two docks many times a day and servicing most of the towns around Lake Atitlán, and many of the teachers of the department (state) of Sololá came from San Pedro (but many other teachers from San Pedro remained unemployed). San Pedro has long been known as an Indian town interested in modernization, education, and the acquisition of property; its inhabitants are sometimes referred to as "the Swiss of Sololá."

At the time of this study, somewhat more than half the residents of the town were Catholic, and most of the rest were fundamentalist Protestants. Of the 14 families in this study, 10 were Catholic, and four were Protestant. The families have been residents of this town for many generations, with marriage occurring almost exclusively with other residents of the town. All parents except one among our 14 families were born and raised locally. An increasing number of young people from the town migrate to cities for education or employment; only some return. Parents in four of our families had lived elsewhere for schooling or employment.

Most of the families (10 of 14) lived in compounds involving several other related families sharing a small courtyard and perhaps a water tap. Most homes had a single sleeping room for the family and another room for a kitchen. Family members slept in the same room, with infants in the maternal bed at least until the next child arrived (about 2 years later). Most of the 12–24-month-olds in our sample still nursed (10 of the 14), and only one had nursed less than 3 months.

All but one family had both mother and father living in the same household; four households contained other adult relatives. The families included one to eight children (mean = 3.4). The target children were the youngest in all the families; three mothers were pregnant at the time of the visits. Mothers' ages (sometimes estimated, as adults often do not keep track of their own age) averaged 27 years; fathers were usually a couple of years older. Five families had experienced deaths of children.

Most homes had an electric light and a radio but no other appliances. Most of the fathers (13 of 14) were involved in agriculture, as day laborers or farmers raising cash crops and corn and beans or as merchants marketing agricultural or other products. (The remaining father was a high school–level student who aspired to a middle-class occupation.) The mothers were based at home, preparing food, tending children, and weaving or sewing to bring in money. Infants and toddlers were usually with their mothers or carried on the hip or entertained by siblings or cousins.

Salt Lake

Salt Lake City, a city of half a million people, is the capital of Utah, in the mountain West of the United States. Our sample, like the population of Salt Lake City, is approximately 50% Mormon (six families), and the remainder were Protestant (three), Catholic (two), or Jewish (one) or had no religion (two). Parents in all but two of our 14 families had either come from another state or lived or visited extensively in other states and countries.

Family structure was exclusively nuclear, with both mother and father living in the same household in all the families. Average age of the mothers was 29 years; fathers were usually the same age or a little older. Half the families had kin living in the same city, but only one family had any kin within walking distance. The number of children ranged from one to four per family, with an average of 1.7. The target children were the youngest in all but one family; three of the mothers were pregnant. Infants and children slept in a separate room from parents, sometimes in the same room as a sibling. None of the 12–24-month-olds of our sample were still nursing; half of them had never nursed or had stopped before 3 months of age.

Family occupations were middle and upper middle class; among the fathers were a medical student and medical residents, a lawyer, a banker, a minister, a certified public accountant, an engineer, a night watchman, a musician, and small businessmen and business employees. Most of the mothers had full- or part-time jobs outside the home, holding such positions as secretary, bookkeeper, teacher, photographer, bank teller, and technical writer. Five of the 14 mothers were at home full time with their children. The children who were not at home with their mothers were tended regularly by grandmothers (four) or unrelated baby-sitters (four) or spent the whole day at a day-care center (one).

Differences between the Communities in Age Segregation

The San Pedro toddlers' nighttime did not involve segregation from the social life in which they participated by day, whereas most of the Salt Lake toddlers spent the night alone, with objects taking the place of human companions. Eleven of the Salt Lake City toddlers slept in a room by themselves, and the remaining three shared a room, but not a bed, with a young sibling. All but one of the San Pedro toddlers slept in the same bed with their mothers (in a room with father or siblings as well); the other one had her own cot in her parents' room. To make the nightly transition to sleeping alone, 10 of the Salt Lake toddlers had extensive bedtime routines, and 11 used attachment objects such as a bottle, toy, or blanket. In contrast, none of the San Pedro toddlers had extensive bedtime routines, and only the one with her own cot used attachment objects to sleep with. (For further discussion of issues of independence and interdependence in toddlers' sleeping arrangements in San Pedro and Salt Lake, see Morelli, Rogoff, Oppenheim, & Goldsmith, 1992.)

During the daytime, the toddlers from the two communities also differed in their access to adult economic and social activities. All the San Pedro toddlers were cared for at home, where all but one of the mothers were involved in some economic activity (weaving or embroidery for sale or small commerce). All the Salt Lake toddlers spent their days in the company of people who were not engaged in economic activity other than the care of children (half in child-care institutions or in the homes of nonrelatives hired to care for them, the other half at home or in the home of an adult relative charged with their care). The structure of parents' days and of their homes makes it difficult for Salt Lake children to observe and participate in adult economic and social activities (other than eavesdropping on the available side of phone calls). This contrasts with the availability of both economic and adult social activities in the homes and courtyards of the San Pedro toddlers. (For further study of the opportunities of young children to observe and participate in adult activities in San Pedro, Salt Lake, Boston, and Zaire, see Morelli, Rogoff, & Angelillo, 1992.)

Differences between the Communities in Goals of Development

Differences between the communities in means of guided participation involve variation in the skills and values that are promoted according to cultural goals of maturity, which vary in keeping with the communities' differences in institutions and related practices and technologies.

Differences in community values appeared in the mothers' reports regarding the pace of their children's development and their own roles in teaching the children. The Salt Lake mothers indicated devoting more effort to advancing the pace of their children's development; 10 of 14 reported that they instructed the child in walking, talking, or helping around the house. In contrast, the San Pedro mothers reported that the children learned to walk and talk by watching others or with parental encouragement; only two of the 14 reported that they taught these skills. Although mothers in both communities were proud of their children's achievements, the Salt Lake mothers appeared to be more concerned with milestones and to consider themselves more responsible for the children's rate of development. One Salt Lake mother, who had devised an extensive curriculum of games to teach her 17-month-old to read letters and to count, commented proudly that "the object permanence has definitely come."

There were marked differences in the infant milestones that had been reached by the toddlers in the two communities. Four of the San Pedro toddlers were toilet trained, and two others were in the process; none of the Salt Lake toddlers were toilet trained, and only one was in the process. Only half the San Pedro toddlers were walking steadily, and three had not yet begun to walk; all the Salt Lake toddlers were skilled in walking. In San Pedro, most of the toddlers were reported to speak three to six words, four were reported to speak seven or more words, and one was reported to combine words. In Salt Lake, most of the children were reported to be speaking a number of words (four were reported to speak three to six words, five to speak seven or more words, and five were reported to be combining words). It is important to note that, with few exceptions, all children in both communities do become toilet trained and skilled in walking and talking.

There were also marked community differences in children's household responsibilities. San Pedro children began to make a real contribution to household work at age 4–6 years (tending infants, delivering messages and running errands around town, helping with meals and agricultural work; see Fig. 3) and were valuable and competent assistants by 8–10 years (making meals, weaving, supervising the household or family shop in the parents' absence, tending crops). In contrast, although Salt Lake children had a few chores at those ages, they played a smaller and less skilled role in household and economic functioning.

Likewise, there were differences between communities in the economic value of the chores in which the mothers reported that their toddler had begun to participate. Three of the 14 San Pedro toddlers took part in economic activities of the adult world by running errands to buy bread at a corner shop or trying to weave; none of the Salt Lake toddlers did so. Such differences undoubtedly relate to the complexity of community layouts and technology, with San Pedro toddlers and children having access to more understandable objects of household work and to the variety of settings of adult activity. The Salt Lake City toddlers (six of 14) more often tried to help use household machines such as vacuum cleaners and dishwashers that are less obvious in their functioning; they also lacked the freedom of movement in their community that the San Pedro toddlers had.

There were large community differences in familiarity with schooling that we argue relate both to the middle-class children's lack of opportunity to participate in adult activities and to the patterns of communication with caregivers that we describe in the next section. In both communities, school-

a

Fig. 3.—By age 5 or 6, San Pedro children provide a great deal of help with household work, including (*a*) tending babies and (*b*) bringing firewood.

ing is highly valued. However, schooling is a foreign institution in San Pedro (originating with the national government) that leads to access to economic opportunities that differ from those available to most San Pedro adults, often removing children from the town both for schooling and for later employment. Although there are local schools (through the ninth grade at the time of our observations), many families that opt for schooling beyond the sixth grade send their children to boarding schools in distant cities. For the parents' generation in our San Pedro sample, schooling beyond the sixth grade was regarded as extensive. The fathers in our families had completed an average of five grades and the mothers three grades, with one father and three mothers having never attended school.

The average amount of schooling in San Pedro is increasing rapidly, and some parents attempt to prepare their toddlers for school by speaking to them in Spanish. (Schooling is in Spanish, the national language, although the native language is a Mayan language.) In our sample, four sets

b

of parents frequently addressed the toddler in Spanish, and five others did so sometimes; the remaining five families spoke to their toddlers only in Mayan, as was traditional. As would be expected, these differences between families in the language used with toddlers were related to parents' schooling. (At the end of this chapter, we explore other differences in the discourse patterns within San Pedro that were associated with variation in mothers' schooling.)

The middle-class parents in our Salt Lake sample had spent many years in school and expected their children to do likewise. Fathers averaged 17 years of schooling; mothers averaged 15 years. All had completed high school. Several of the toddlers attended playgroups a few days a week for access to peer interaction and preparation for preschool; children in this community generally go to private preschool at age 3 or 4. Older children's primary responsibility is their own schoolwork. The language and discourse practices of school are related to those in the homes, where the practices of schooling have been regarded for several generations as closely related to occupational and life success in adulthood.

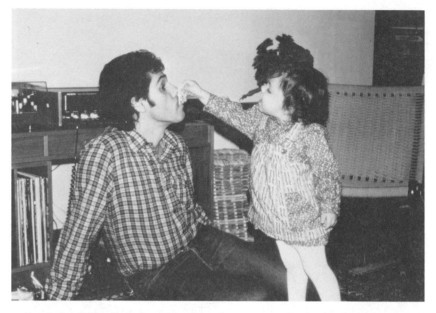

Fig. 4.—A Salt Lake father enters into play as a peer, sipping his daughter's pretend cup of tea.

Preparation of toddlers for success in school is seen as an important part of parents' roles and may relate to parents' concern with rate of achievement of milestones in infancy as well as to discourse patterns between parents and toddlers, such as parents entering into play with their toddlers as peers (see Fig. 4). All the Salt Lake mothers reported that they were often their toddler's playmate; most reported that the father also served as a playmate to the toddler.

In contrast, all but one of the San Pedro mothers reported that neither parent acted as a playmate to the toddler; the toddlers' playmates were other children. Several San Pedro mothers laughed with embarrassment at the idea of entering into play with their toddlers, as this is the role of other children and occasionally grandparents. When a toddler is playing, reported the San Pedro mothers, it is time for a mother to get her work done. Although San Pedro parents may tickle and jounce their babies affectionately, they seldom play as peers with their toddlers.

We expected these differences in children's participation in community economic structure and their age segregation, schooling, and parent-child roles to be visible in our videotaped observations of caregiver-child communication and shared problem solving.

OBSERVATIONS OF GUIDED PARTICIPATION: NOVEL OBJECTS

Preliminary Analyses

Because we did not have predictions for gender and age differences, we limited our consideration of main effects (across the two communities) and interactions involving gender or age (by community) to those reaching a criterion of $p < .01$ in significance level in order to avoid overinterpreting the number of differences that could appear by chance. The only two gender or age differences that reached this criterion were the following. (1) Girls were more likely than boys to share their attention simultaneously among several events at once, $F(1, 24) = 8.2$, $p = .008$, which is consistent with impressions that girls are sensitive to social subtleties (usually at least one of the competing events was social). (2) Older children (18–24 months) used more words than younger children (12–17 months), $F(1, 24) = 11.3$, $p = .003$, which is consistent with research on language development.[7]

There was no significant difference between San Pedro and Salt Lake in the number of interactional moves made by the toddler during the episodes, indicating that the toddlers were roughly equally involved in the interactions; they averaged between 10 and 20 interactional moves in both communities.

In both communities, the toddlers always had at least one adult partner in the episode (mother, father, or another adult). In addition, the San Pedro toddlers had responsible child partners (aged 4–13 years) in an average of 34% of the episodes; this occurred in an average of 3% of the Salt Lake episodes (significantly less than in San Pedro, $t[13] = 3.0$, $p < .05$). Inclusion of responsible child partners in analyses of caregivers did not change the pattern of results. All analyses presented below include responsible child partners if they were involved, except for the conversational peer variables, which were analyzed separately for adult and for responsible child partners in case toddlers acted as conversational peers with child caregivers but not with adults.

---

[7] We also examined age and gender main effects in an analysis of variance that included the data from all four communities. There were no gender differences with $p < .01$; the few age differences were that more mock excitement was employed by caregivers with younger children, $F(1, 54) = 8.1$, $p = .006$, more simplification by means of gesture was used by caregivers with older children, $F(1, 54) = 8.9$, $p = .004$, older children more frequently sought assistance, $F(1, 54) = 7.8$, $p = .007$, and older children used more words, $F(1, 54) = 10.0$, $p = .003$. These differences make sense but are not particularly interesting in their own right.

Cultural Similarities in Guided Participation

In this section, we focus on processes of guided participation that we propose are similar across widely different cultural communities: *creating bridges* to make connections to new ideas and interpretations and *structuring children's participation* in activities through adjusting opportunities for their involvement and through supporting and structuring their involvement in activities.

Creating Bridges

One indication of bridging between children's and caregivers' perspectives is their mutual engagement in the same agenda, whether involvement is symmetrical or is arranged with one or the other partner taking a leadership role. In almost all the novel object episodes, the toddlers were closely involved with their caregivers through engaging with the same agenda (e.g., caregiver and child working the object together or caregiver attempting to assist child, who attempted to work the object with this help). Such mutual involvement was the case for an average of 89% of the episodes for San Pedro and 81% for Salt Lake families (the difference is not significant).

In addition, almost all caregivers provided bridging by indicating to the toddlers the nature of the activity with the object, orienting the children in an average of 99% of the episodes in San Pedro and 96% of the episodes in Salt Lake (again, the difference is not significant). Thus, almost all caregivers provided orientation, bridging their own and their toddler's understanding of the activity.

Structuring

The toddlers and caregivers together structured the toddlers' involvement in working the novel objects. Most caregivers adjusted the object or its position to facilitate the toddlers' efforts, divided or simplified the task, and handled difficult moves. This was the case in an average of 93% of the San Pedro episodes and 87% of the Salt Lake episodes (N.S.). Figures 5 and 6 illustrate the structuring that occurred in the interactions of a San Pedro family and a Salt Lake family with the jumping-jack puppet.

Almost all the toddlers in both communities were also involved in one way or another in structuring the activity: they introduced information or structure (in an average of 33% of the episodes in San Pedro and 29% of the episodes in Salt Lake, N.S.), sought clarification by social referencing using gaze (51% and 16%, respectively; the difference is discussed below), sought involvement (89% and 79%, respectively, N.S.), and sought assistance (43% and 33%, respectively, N.S.).

These findings support the proposition that bridging and structuring are widespread in differing communities. At the same time, there were important differences in goals of development for the children and in the means of communication used by caregivers and children in the two communities.

Cultural Variation in Guided Participation

Means of Communication and Instruction

Verbal and nonverbal communication.—Consistent with many cross-cultural studies, there were differences in both verbal and nonverbal communication in the two communities. Salt Lake caregivers spoke more to their toddlers, whereas San Pedro caregivers more frequently used several forms of nonverbal communication.

The amount of speech addressed by Salt Lake caregivers to their toddlers averaged four to nine sentences, whereas San Pedro caregivers averaged slightly below three sentences, $t(18) = 2.3$, $p < .05$ (for means and standard deviations, see Table 1; graphs explained in Chap. V also display the contrasts between the San Pedro and the Salt Lake data). In San Pedro, there were six times as many episodes having three or fewer sentences from caregivers than in Salt Lake, whereas twice as many episodes had more than 10 sentences in Salt Lake than in San Pedro.

In their turn, the San Pedro toddlers were less talkative; they averaged less than one word per episode, whereas the Salt Lake toddlers averaged one to three words per episode. Almost twice as many San Pedro as Salt Lake episodes involved no words spoken by the toddlers; in three times as many Salt Lake as San Pedro episodes, the toddler used one or more phrases. Since there was a significant main effect for age of toddlers in their amount of talking, we included age in the analyses of the difference between communities. The age (younger vs. older toddlers) × community (San Pedro vs. Salt Lake) ANOVA yielded a difference between communities, $F(1, 24) = 4.9$, $p < .04$ (for means and standard deviations, see Table 1).

We examined the extent to which the two communities varied in the means of communication used to orient the child to the activity and to simplify the child's involvement in managing the objects. Most caregivers used both verbal and nonverbal means, but still with differences in prevalence between the two communities. There were no differences between the communities in the proportion of episodes in which caregivers provided any verbal orientation or verbal simplification of the children's involvement (most did) or simplified the child's involvement by adjusting the object or the child's hands (most did; see Table 1). However, the San Pedro caregivers more frequently used nonverbal means to orient the toddlers, $t(19) = 2.3$,

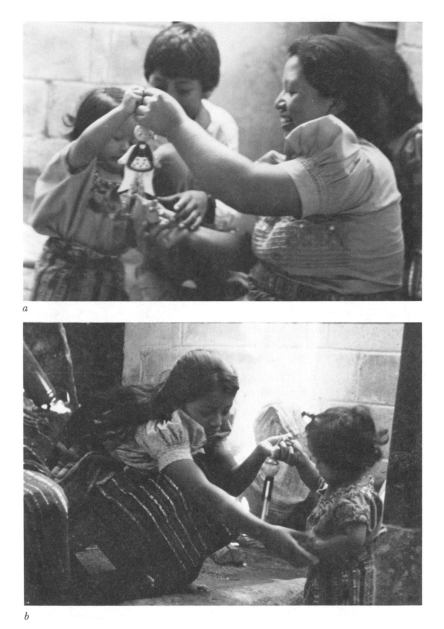

a

b

FIG. 5.—*a*, A San Pedro mother helps her 15-month-old daughter manage the top string of the jumping jack, as she helps the toddler grasp the bottom string. (Note the contribution of the older boy too.) *b*, Soon, the toddler takes the jumping jack to her older sister, who also helps her hold the top string while reaching for the bottom string. (Holding onto both strings at once and working them was challenging for toddlers.) *c*, The older sister devised a simplification of the task that the toddler employs with her mother as they make the jumping jack's arms and legs dance.

c

$p < .05$, and more frequently simplified the toddlers' involvement using gestures, $t(25) = 2.6$, $p < .01$, and communicative gaze, touch, posture, or timing cues, $t(13) = 4.7$, $p < .001$. Communicative gaze, touch, posture, or timing cues were used in 37% of the San Pedro episodes (and several types were often used in the same episode); such communication was almost non-existent in Salt Lake. An example of the use of such cues in San Pedro is provided by a mother who helped her 19-month-old work the jumping jack (a marionette that kicks its legs when its bottom string is pulled and its top string held):

> The mother used a firm manner of placing the child's hands on the strings to mark the importance of holding firmly onto them, positioning the jumping-jack toy in a position that indicated to the child to hold the bottom string lower, and tapping the child gently on the arm, indicating not to pull the string so hard.

This is consistent with the expectation of greater use of nonverbal means of communication in San Pedro and balances the greater extent of talk by the Salt Lake caregivers. San Pedro caregivers appeared to use a more complex conventional system of gestural and gaze, touch, posture, or timing communication than the Salt Lake caregivers, with the possibility of expressing more complex ideas nonverbally in San Pedro.

a

FIG. 6.—*a*, A Salt Lake mother encourages her 21-month-old son's involvement with the jumping jack with mock excitement. *b*, She supports his operation of the bottom string and simplifies the task by holding the top string for him.

The observations of skilled use of nonverbal communication fit with casual observations of its extensive use among adults in San Pedro. It is also consistent with anecdotal observations from our laboratory of the difficulty experienced by middle-class Caucasian coders in noticing these forms of communication; training such coders has routinely required teaching them to attend to such cues, while, for Native North and Central American coders, such cues are immediately noticed and "legible."

On their part, the San Pedro toddlers also used more gaze, touch, posture, or timing communication than did the Salt Lake toddlers, $t(15) = 4.2, p < .001$, in their efforts to seek greater assistance from their caregivers. Such communication occurred in a fifth of the San Pedro episodes and in almost none of the Salt Lake episodes (see Table 1). The toddlers from the two communities did not differ in the frequency of use of verbal or gestural means, calling to their caregivers or holding an object out for assistance.

b

In addition, the San Pedro toddlers were more likely to seek clarification of ambiguous situations through gaze, $t(25) = 4.4$, $p < .0001$, doing so more than three times as often as the Salt Lake toddlers (for means, see Table 1; for an example of a San Pedro toddler seeking clarification through gaze, see Fig. 7).[8]

The findings thus indicate that Salt Lake caregivers and toddlers used verbal communication to a greater extent than did San Pedro caregivers and toddlers, who in turn used nonverbal communication to a greater extent.

Explanation and demonstration.—The literature suggests that instructional interactions in middle-class Western communities involve explanation out of the context of ongoing activity (i.e., explanation of nonpresent phenomena, as is common in schools) and that those in many non-Western

[8] We looked for the use of verbal, gestural, and touch, posture, or timing means of seeking clarification, but these were very rare.

TABLE 1

	San Pedro	Salt Lake	Dhol-Ki-Patti	Keçiören
Talk to child (3 = 1–3 sentences; 4 = 4–9 sentences; 5 = 10+ sentences)	3.87 (.94)	4.51 (.43)	3.40 (1.34)	4.81 (.33)
Child's talk (0 = no words; 1 = 1–3 words; 2 = 4+ words; 3 = 1–3 phrases; 4 = 4+ phrases)	.71 (1.01)	1.30 (.95)	.07 (.15)	1.11 (1.03)
Caregiver orients child verbally (proportion of episodes)	.63 (.29)	.74 (.27)	.39 (.38)	.80 (.19)
Caregiver orients child nonverbally (proportion of episodes)	.99 (.05)	.91 (.10)	.91 (.27)	.96 (.09)
Caregiver simplifies verbally (proportion of episodes)	.71 (.31)	.69 (.24)	.45 (.37)	.89 (.15)
Caregiver simplifies by adjustment of object or child's hands (proportion of episodes)	.91 (.13)	.80 (.25)	.67 (.34)	.89 (.15)
Caregiver simplifies by gesture (proportion of episodes)	.61 (.23)	.37 (.26)	.43 (.34)	.47 (.17)
Caregiver simplifies by gaze, touch, posture, or timing cues (proportion of episodes)	.37 (.28)	.01 (.05)	.40 (.41)	.01 (.05)
Child seeks assistance verbally (proportion of episodes)	.17 (.22)	.19 (.29)	0 (0)	.09 (.17)
Child seeks assistance with gestures (proportion of episodes)	.40 (.28)	.30 (.32)	.31 (.36)	.13 (.17)
Child seeks assistance with gaze, touch, posture, or timing cues (proportion of episodes)	.20 (.16)	.01 (.05)	.17 (.31)	.01 (.05)
Child seeks clarification with gaze (proportion of episodes)	.51 (.23)	.16 (.19)	[a]	[a]

[a] This variable was dropped from analysis in these two communities (see Chap. III).

Fig. 7.—An 18-month-old San Pedro girl references her mother, seeking clarification through gaze regarding what she should do with a novel object.

communities involve demonstration in the context of an ongoing activity. Owing to our observational situation, most of the talk with these young children does not involve explanation out of context because it was related to the ongoing shared activity.[9] Therefore, we focus on caregivers' references to similarities between the novel object activity and other activities (our variable *extending to other situations*) to examine the expectation of greater likelihood of explanation out of context in Salt Lake and more extensive demonstration in San Pedro.

Extending to other situations involved statements that drew connections with analogous situations—for example, referring to the embroidery hoop as being "like Mommy's bracelet" or to the jumping-jack doll as "dancing!" or saying, "Peek-a-boo," when hiding the puppet in and popping it back out of the cone. These statements refer to the situation at hand in terms of another system of activity. There were significant differences between communities, with the Salt Lake caregivers twice as likely as the San Pedro caregivers to provide such explanation, $t(25) = 3.2$, $p < .01$ (see Table 2).

[9] We did code a subcategory of talk that included all talk by the caregiver related to characteristics or actions of the novel object or the dressing situation; however, since this constituted almost all the talk to the child, we do not consider it further.

TABLE 2

EXPLANATION AND DEMONSTRATION IN NOVEL OBJECTS EPISODES:
MEANS (and Standard Deviations)

	San Pedro	Salt Lake	Dhol-Ki-Patti	Keçiören
Extending to other situations (proportion of episodes)	.24 (.18)	.47 (.20)	.31 (.36)	.61 (.28)
Demonstration before child participates (0 = none; 1 = brief; 2 = moderate; 3 = extensive)	1.80 (.64)	1.11 (.48)	1.21 (.84)	1.13 (.45)
Demonstration during child participation (as in previous entry) ...	1.96 (.68)	1.61 (.59)	1.70 (.97)	2.00 (.45)
Directing attention to process (proportion of episodes)	.71 (.30)	.37 (.22)	.57 (.41)	.69 (.24)
Turning task over to child (proportion of episodes)	.41 (.20)	.16 (.21)	.67 (.36)	.14 (.18)

There were also differences between the communities in the amount of demonstration given children. Our aim in separating the episodes according to when the child began to participate in the activity was to see if there were community differences in the extent of advance presentation. Before the children began to participate, caregivers in San Pedro provided more demonstration than did those in Salt Lake, $t(24) = 3.2$, $p < .01$ (see Table 2), but, once the child began to participate, there was no significant difference in the amount of further demonstration given. However, it is worth noting that San Pedro caregivers provided at least as much demonstration during participation as did Salt Lake caregivers, ruling out the possibility that the two groups just demonstrate at different points in the interaction.

Consistent with the pattern of demonstration by the San Pedro caregivers were two other aspects of their communication: San Pedro caregivers were twice as likely to direct the child's attention to critical aspects of the process as they demonstrated (often saying "Like this" or "Did you see?"), $t(23) = 3.4$, $p < .01$, and to turn the task over to the child (often with a statement indicating that the child is ready, e.g., "Now you do it"), $t(25) = 3.3$, $p < .01$ (see Table 2). Thus, the pattern in San Pedro was to provide an introductory demonstration, which included directing the child's attention to critical aspects of the procedure, and then to give the child the responsibility to carry out the activity.

Adult-Child Roles in Teaching and Learning

Adults serving as children's play partners or conversational peers enter the world of children in ways that may reflect cultural differences in whether adults or children are responsible for learning. They may provide children with lessons that simplify adult systems of knowledge in contrived situations. A need for such adult regulation and motivation may be related to the fact that children in middle-class communities have fewer opportunities to observe and participate in adult activities and thereby learn through their own involvement.

Status equals in play.—Consistent with the reports of Salt Lake mothers that they often served as their toddler's playmate and with the reports of San Pedro mothers that they did not regard being their toddler's playmate as part of their role, our observations during the novel object episodes showed differences in frequency of acting as playmate. Salt Lake caregivers often served as playmates for their toddlers, going beyond encouraging the child's play to acting as playmates themselves in almost half the episodes; this seldom occurred in San Pedro, $t(16) = 4.4$, $p < .001$. In San Pedro, the mothers sometimes recruited one of their older children to play with the toddler, supervising the sibling play and sometimes directing the older child in helping the toddler work the objects. Thus, the San Pedro mothers were not uninvolved with their toddlers' play, but they acted as supervisors rather than as playmates.

Adults teaching versus supporting children learning.—Salt Lake caregivers often placed themselves on the child's level by speaking with the children as peers, and they also attempted to motivate and manage the child's learning. San Pedro caregivers maintained a difference of status while instructing their children and maintained a readiness to assist whenever the toddlers indicated a need for help. The differences are consistent with the Salt Lake children being treated as the object of teaching and the San Pedro children being responsible for learning.

In most of the Salt Lake episodes, adults interacted with toddlers as conversational peers, asking their opinions, responding to their vocalizations as conversation, and providing openings for equal dialogic exchanges (see Fig. 8); the San Pedro toddlers were seldom treated as conversational peers, $t(23) = 5.3$, $p < .001$ (see Table 3).[10]

In their turn, the Salt Lake toddlers took a conversational peer role in over half the episodes, offering comments and initiating optional conversation, but the San Pedro toddlers seldom took a conversational peer role with

---

[10] The San Pedro caregivers more often provided instruction that was structured as a lecture without an attempt to involve the toddler (21% of the episodes); this never occurred in the Salt Lake episodes.

Fɪɢ. 8.—A Salt Lake mother converses with her 12-month-old daughter as a peer

adults, $t(25) = 3.5$, $p < .001$.[11] Although the toddlers in both communities interacted reciprocally with their parents in almost all episodes—through joint action and communication in the context of carrying out the activities—the Salt Lake families were distinguished by the use of peer conversational dialogue.

Many episodes with the Salt Lake toddlers involved talk that can be seen as lessons in language use (whether self-conscious or intuitive) in which utterances served no regulative function in the ongoing activity. Such language lessons seldom occurred in the San Pedro episodes. The Salt Lake City caregivers used marked babytalk intonations in almost all episodes; the San Pedro caregivers did so in less than a third of their episodes, $t(16) = 5.4$, $p < .0001$ (see Table 3). The Salt Lake caregivers provided vocabulary lessons by labeling objects, requesting labels, providing running commentary on events, expanding children's speech, and playing language games often involving test questions that requested information that caregivers already knew ("What's that?" or "Where's the baby's eyes?"). Figure 9 shows a mother and toddler focusing on language lessons.

[11] We also looked for the presence of conversational peer dialogue between toddlers and caregiving child partners who were involved with the toddlers in a third of the episodes in San Pedro; there was none. In Salt Lake, caregiving child partners were involved in very few of our observations.

TABLE 3

ADULT TEACHING VERSUS SUPPORT FOR CHILD LEARNING IN NOVEL OBJECTS EPISODES:
MEANS (and Standard Deviations)

	San Pedro	Salt Lake	Dhol-Ki-Patti	Keçiören
Caregiver acts as playmate (proportion of episodes)	.07	.47	.24	.63
	(.13)	(.32)	(.36)	(.32)
Adult converses with child as peer (proportion of episodes)	.19	.79	.39	.83
	(.35)	(.24)	(.44)	(.17)
Child converses with adult as peer (proportion of episodes)	.16	.57	.20	.60
	(.33)	(.29)	(.36)	(.41)
Caregiver uses babytalk (proportion of episodes)	.30	.93	.38	.89
	(.41)	(.15)	(.49)	(.23)
Caregiver vocabulary lesson (5 types possible for max score = 5)	.60	2.16	.58	2.23
	(.88)	(.86)	(.87)	(1.00)
Child vocabulary lesson (3 types possible for max score = 3)	.14	.46	.07	.40
	(.23)	(.47)	(.19)	(.36)
Caregiver mock excitement (proportion of episodes)	.13	.74	.32	.74
	(.22)	(.29)	(.41)	(.24)
Caregiver praise (proportion of episodes)	.04	.44	.05	.19
	(.09)	(.31)	(.18)	(.17)
Caregiver poised ready to help (proportion of episodes)	.81	.23	.65	.60
	(.24)	(.23)	(.38)	(.21)
Caregiver overrules child (proportion of child refusal/insistence episodes)	.14	.52	[a]	.69
	(.29)	(.45)		(.34)

[a] This variable was dropped from analysis in this community (see Chap. III).

The Salt Lake caregivers averaged two of the five kinds of vocabulary lesson per episode; the San Pedro caregivers averaged less than one, $t(25)$ = 4.7, $p < .0001$. The relative frequency of each type of vocabulary lesson was as follows: caregivers labeled objects in 50% of the episodes in Salt Lake and 16% in San Pedro, requested labels in 31% and 6% of the episodes, provided running commentary on events in 70% and 21% of the episodes, expanded child speech in 44% and 13% of the episodes, and engaged in language games in 20% and 4% of the episodes, respectively. The Salt Lake toddlers themselves participated more frequently in vocabulary lessons (primarily labeling objects but also requesting labels or participating in language games) than did the San Pedro toddlers, $t(18)$ = 2.3, $p < .05$ (see Table 3).

FIG. 9.—During a moment of picture book reading, a Salt Lake mother and toddler engage in language lessons, labeling objects and playing language games involving test questions.

Consistent with the notion that Salt Lake caregivers organized instruction, they more frequently attempted to motivate their children's involvement in the working of the toys through mock excitement when beginning to work with each toy (see Fig. 6a above) as well as through praise of the children's efforts and performances. Most of the Salt Lake episodes involved mock excitement, but few in San Pedro involved such motivational efforts, $t(24) = 6.4$, $p < .0001$; almost half the Salt Lake caregivers used praise to reward their children, but this almost never occurred in San Pedro, $t(15) = 4.7$, $p < .001$ (see Table 3).[12]

Examples of most of these discourse practices are available in the inter-

[12] The Salt Lake toddlers also more frequently praised themselves or showed off their efforts (in an average of 20% of the episodes; SD = .22) than did the San Pedro toddlers (3% of the episodes; SD = .07, $t[15] = 2.7$, $p < .01$).

action of a 21-month-old Salt Lake boy and his mother, which took place while exploring the jar containing the peewee doll. The mother and child conversed as peers, the mother attempted to motivate the child's involvement through mock excitement, and both partners engaged in vocabulary lessons (requesting labeling, labeling, running commentary, expanding child speech, and language games):

> Sandy's mother held the jar up and chirped excitedly, "What is it? What's inside?" and then pointed to the peewee doll inside, "Is that a little person?" When Sandy pulled down on the jar, she suggested, "Can you take the lid off?"
> Sandy inspected the round knob on top and said, "Da ball."
> "Da ball, yeah," his mother confirmed. "Pull the lid," she encouraged, and demonstrated pulling on the knob, "Can you pull?" Sandy put his hand on hers, and they pulled the lid off together triumphantly. "What's inside?" asked his mother, and took the peewee out, "Who is that?"
> Sandy reached for the lid, and his mother provided running commentary, "OK, you put the lid back on." And when Sandy exclaimed "Oh!" his mother repeated "Oh!" after him. When Sandy lost interest, his mother asked with mock disappointment, "Oh, you don't want to play anymore?" and suggested, "We could make him play peek-a-boo."
> When Sandy took the peewee out, she asked, "Where did she go?" and sang, "There, she's all gone," as she covered the peewee with her hands. "Aaall gone."

In contrast, the San Pedro caregivers were more responsive to their children's own efforts to understand and work the objects. They were poised in readiness to assist the toddlers in an average of 81% of the episodes, contrasting with 23% of the episodes with the Salt Lake caregivers, $t(25) = 6.5, p < .0001$ (see Table 3). Being poised ready to help is a responsive way of assisting the children that leaves the pace and direction of children's efforts up to them. (For an illustration of a San Pedro mother poised ready to help her toddler, see Fig. 10.)

An example of the responsive attentiveness and readiness to assist (and sharing of attention) is apparent in the interactions of a 20-month-old San Pedro boy and his mother:

> As the interviewer subtly showed the jar to his mother, Juan did not miss a move. And when the interviewer handed Juan's 4-year-old brother the embroidery hoop, both Juan and his mother monitored this as they handled the jar together. The mother shook the jar, pointing to the peewee inside, "Look at the doll . . . how it is moving!" and Juan watched, then grasped and shook the jar.

Fɪɢ. 10.—A San Pedro mother sits poised ready to help her 15-month-old put together a nesting doll. Note how the mother maintains both hands in a posture of readiness to assist.

When Juan enthusiastically showed the jar to his father—"Papa! . . . Baby!"—his father (who had been demonstrating the embroidery hoop to the brother) smiled and told Juan to take it out.

Juan turned toward his mother and shook the jar—"Baby!"—and put the jar into his mother's hand. Although she was involved in an adult conversation, she received the jar and shook it for Juan.

But Juan pointed at the lid, tapping it with his index finger, to request his mother to remove the lid, as she bounced the jar in her hands. When she noticed what Juan was doing (as she continued conversing), she took the lid off and held the jar open long enough for him to take out the peewee, then closed the jar and held it available in front of him. The interaction continued, with Juan working the jar and his mother ready to assist as she also attended to the ongoing conversation.

When Juan turned around again to show his father the peewee—"Papa! . . . Baby"—his father repeated "Baby" as he simultaneously attended to the adult conversation and demonstrated the hoop to the brother.

Juan smiled and turned to examine the peewee, then touched the peewee to the jar that his mother held, with a quiet request vocalization. She glanced down and understood what Juan wanted. Juan proceeded to work the jar, lid, and peewee with his mother's assistance, smoothly contributed as she attended simultaneously to adult conversation.

Responsiveness as respect for autonomy.—The responsiveness of the San Pedro caregivers is especially important to note because, in informal discussion of our results, many middle-class U.S. scholars have indicated an assumption that, since Salt Lake caregivers are playmates and "child oriented" and San Pedro toddlers are more interdependent with a group, the San Pedro toddlers must be left out, dependent, treated mechanically, or deprived of autonomy. This is not so, as is demonstrated by the greater readiness of San Pedro caregivers to help according to the toddlers' need rather than organizing the toddlers' motivation and learning.

Our codings of whether the caregivers responded to the toddler's insistence or refusal to do something by acceding to the toddlers' wishes, or by insisting or refusing in return, may also reflect the San Pedro caregivers' tendency to accord autonomy and final responsibility for decisions to the children. Although the San Pedro toddlers were about twice as likely as the Salt Lake toddlers to refuse or insist (in an average of 63% [SD = .25] as opposed to 33% [SD = .29] of the episodes, $t[25] = 3.0, p < .05$), San Pedro caregivers were much *less* likely to try to overrule the toddlers' insistence or refusal by responding with insistence or refusal of their own, $t(16) = 2.4$, $p < .05$. The Salt Lake caregivers more often tried to supersede the children's will, not accepting children's refusal or insistence on a course of action. They went beyond coaxing (which occurred to similar extents in the two communities), attempting to force the children, an action that by San Pedro standards (expressed in conversations) amounts to a lack of respect for the children's autonomy.

An example of San Pedro parents trying to persuade but stopping short of forcing a child to comply occurred when 18-month-old Roberto did not want to put on his cloth diaper and trousers:

> First his mother tried coaxing, then bribing with false promises. "Let's put on your diaper. . . . Let's go to Grandma's. . . . We're going to do an errand." This did not work, and the mother invited Roberto to nurse, as she swiftly slipped the diaper on him with the father's assistance. The father announced, "It's over!" and as a distraction offered Roberto the ball that we had brought.
>
> The mother continued the offer of the toy, with her voice reflecting increasing exasperation that the child was wiggling and not standing to facilitate putting on his pants. Her voice softened as Roberto became interested in the ball, and she increased the stakes: "Do you want another toy?" Roberto listened to both parents say, "Then put on your pants." They continued to try to talk Roberto into cooperating and handed him various objects, which Roberto enjoyed. But still he stubbornly refused to cooperate with dressing. They left him alone for a while. When his father asked if he was ready, Roberto pouted, "Nono!" After a bit, the mother told Roberto that she was leaving and waved

goodbye. "Are you going with me?" Roberto sat quietly with a worried look. "Then put on your pants, put on your pants to go up the hill." Roberto stared into space, seeming to consider the alternatives. His mother started to walk away. "OK then, I'm going. Goodbye." Roberto started to cry, and his father persuaded, "Put on your pants then!" and his mother asked, "Are you going with me?"

Roberto looked down worriedly, one arm outstretched in a half take-me gesture. "Come on, then," his mother urged as she offered the pants, and Roberto let his father lift him to a stand and cooperated in putting his legs into the pants and in standing to have them fastened. His mother did not intend to leave; instead, she suggested that Roberto dance for the audience. Roberto did a baby version of a traditional dance, looking up slightly poutily at the interviewer.

These San Pedro parents' persuasive and distracting tactics worked. Although their promises and threats were not carried out, the parents seemed to maintain a boundary of not forcefully intervening against the child's will.

These observations are consistent with others that we made in San Pedro that suggest that there is a respect for personal autonomy that cannot be breached even to achieve something that is regarded as necessary for the well-being of another. (For example, family members have been observed not to hold a child against her will for a medical procedure—"She doesn't want to.") Similar observations of respect for the autonomy of an individual's decisions in communities that stress interdependence have been made among Kaluli in Papua New Guinea ("One can never compel another to act. One can appeal and try to move others to act, or assert what one wants" [Schieffelin, 1991, p. 245]), in Navajo families and peer groups (Deyhle, 1991; Ellis & Gauvain, 1992; Lamphere, 1977), and among the Inuit (Briggs, 1991) (see also Lee, 1976).

From these data, and from prior ethnographic study of child-rearing practices in the community (Rogoff, 1976), it is clear that, far from having little say, the San Pedro toddlers are granted a great deal of autonomy. Mosier, Rogoff, and Chavajay (1992) found that San Pedro toddlers have a special status in the family that involves an assumption that they are not willfully negative but rather interdependent with caregivers, which is associated with caregivers respecting toddlers' demands. This contrasts with the assumption of middle-class U.S. families and researchers that infants are willful, independent persons with whom to negotiate, sometimes in battles of the will or tugs-of-war. The San Pedro pattern of status differences between adults and children, accompanied by interdependence with respect for young children's autonomy, provides a challenge to commonly held assumptions in U.S. research regarding the nature both of caregiver-infant relationships and of individuality and independence.

To summarize the pattern of adult-child roles in teaching and learning, the San Pedro caregivers demonstrated the activity and then turned it over to the toddlers, providing further instruction and demonstration in a manner responsive to the children's indications of a need for help. San Pedro toddlers' actions often occurred at their own instigation; they received abundant assistance when they needed it, and their cleverness might receive a pleasant acknowledgment, but it did not result in a public evaluation of intelligence or expressions of praise. The Salt Lake caregivers attempted to motivate learning and structure instruction even to the point of overruling the toddlers' desires, often using mock excitement, praise, play, and peer conversation to draw the children into the adults' lessons.

Learning through Observation

Management of attention.—The literature suggests that, in non-Western cultures in which children learn through participation in ongoing adult activity, children may be keen observers. To examine this possibility, we investigated how the children and their caregivers managed their attention to ongoing events. We were interested in the relative prevalence of three ways to handle competing events: attending to them simultaneously, rapidly alternating attention between them, or appearing unaware of them. These three approaches were rated relative to each other, controlling for differences in the number of competing events in differing families and communities.

We assume that the keen observation necessary for learning in ongoing activities is facilitated by sharing attention among several ongoing events. If children can expect that others will take responsibility for organizing their learning, they need not manage their own attention with such dexterity—they can focus their attention on the activity at hand and count on others to let them know if they are to shift attention.

The San Pedro toddlers were more likely to attend to several events simultaneously (such as working an object with the caregiver and monitoring other conversation, glancing at and being involved with the flow of events) than were the Salt Lake toddlers, who seldom appeared to attend to several events simultaneously, $t(15) = 7.4$, $p < .0001$ (for presentation of these data, see Table 4 and Fig. 11). The Salt Lake toddlers generally attended to one event at a time—their own activity or a joint activity—either by alternating attention between the two or by focusing exclusively on one. They were more likely to appear unaware of ongoing events than were the San Pedro toddlers, $t(24) = 4.4$, $p < .0001$. The relative frequency of the three types of attention management were reversed in the two communities,

TABLE 4

ATTENTION MANAGEMENT AND ENGAGEMENT EMBEDDED IN GROUP IN NOVEL OBJECTS
EPISODES: MEANS (and Standard Deviations)

	San Pedro	Salt Lake	Dhol-Ki-Patti	Keçiören
Child attends simultaneously	1.96	.31	.36	.11
	(.79)	(.25)	(.40)	(.15)
Child attends alternately	1.50	1.64	2.64	2.44
	(.45)	(.72)	(1.29)	(.74)
Child appears unaware of events	1.16	2.30	1.26	1.67
	(.60)	(.77)	(.84)	(.90)
Caregiver attends simultaneously	3.49	.98	1.77	1.04
	(.41)	(.88)	(.84)	(.43)
Caregiver attends alternately	.59	1.35	1.96	2.55
	(.27)	(.87)	(.70)	(.56)
Caregiver appears unaware of events	.13	1.63	.61	.32
	(.22)	(1.00)	(.70)	(.42)
Engagement embedded in group (proportion of episodes)	.53	.10	.41	.14
	(.36)	(.15)	(.39)	(.18)

NOTE.—The three types of attention were rated relative to each other for child and for caregiver, according to the following scale: 0 = never occurred; 1 = sometimes occurred but not as much as some other attentional category; 2 = occurred as much as any other attentional category; 3 = was the primary attentional category; 4 = was used overwhelmingly during the episode.

with San Pedro toddlers attending simultaneously most frequently, then alternating, then being unaware, and Salt Lake toddlers following the opposite order.

The caregivers followed the same pattern as the children. The San Pedro caregivers overwhelmingly attended simultaneously to several events; they were seldom rated as managing their attention in any other fashion (see Table 4 and Fig. 11). That they could pay attention to competing events simultaneously may have been facilitated by devoting verbal channels of communication largely to adult conversation and relying heavily on nonverbal channels—gesture, gaze, touch, posture, and timing communication—with the toddlers. Salt Lake caregivers were much less likely than the San Pedro caregivers to attend simultaneously to several events, $t(18) = 9.7$, $p < .0001$, and more commonly either attended to competing events alternately or appeared unaware of competing events (community differences were significant: alternating attention, $t[15] = 3.1$, $p < .01$; unaware of competing events, $t[14] = 5.5$, $p < .0001$).

The example described above of Juan and his mother handling the jar and peewee illustrates the San Pedro caregivers' simultaneous attention, as Juan's mother assisted him at the same time as contributing to adult conversation and his father simultaneously replied to Juan, monitored adult conversation, and demonstrated the embroidery hoop for Juan's brother.

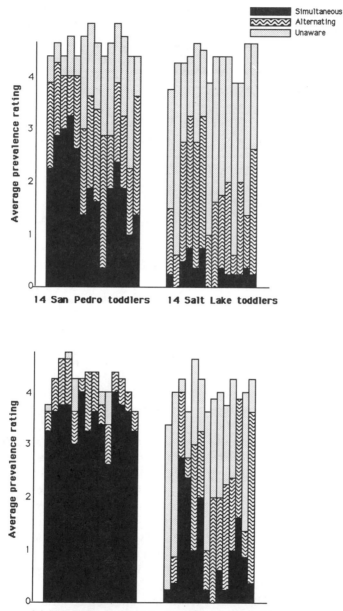

FIG. 11.—Attention management while operating novel objects in San Pedro and Salt Lake. Within the communities, toddlers are arrayed from youngest to oldest girl, then youngest to oldest boy, with caregivers matched.

Juan's parents managed their attention in this manner throughout the novel object and dressing episodes. At one point in the visit, Juan's mother managed four different activities at once, including Juan's activity with an object, the adult conversation, a tussle between two daughters, and a request directed to another child. Throughout the interactions, Juan's mother, like many of the other San Pedro caregivers, kept alert to the possibility of things happening by subtly keeping her eyes moving in a way that we almost never saw with the Salt Lake caregivers. We dubbed this "air-traffic-controller" monitoring to attempt to capture the light movement from one potential activity to another, registering and contributing to all, getting stuck on none.

The same patterns of attention management are seen for both caregivers and children in each community (see Fig. 11). Caregivers in each community were more likely to pay attention to several events simultaneously than were their toddlers (paired sample, $t[13] = 6.9$, $p < .0001$ in San Pedro, $t[13] = 3.6$, $p = .01$ in Salt Lake). However, it is striking that the *toddlers* in San Pedro (like their caregivers) more frequently attended simultaneously to several events than did the *caregivers* in Salt Lake, $t(25) = 3.1$, $p < .01$. Although it seems likely that attending simultaneously to several events requires some skill and learning, by the age of 12–24 months San Pedro children already show the same pattern of attention management as their caregivers. San Pedro toddlers skillfully attended simultaneously on many occasions, and air-traffic-controller monitoring occurred with some San Pedro toddlers, although much less frequently than with their mothers. Similarly, the Salt Lake toddlers followed the same pattern of attention deployment as their caregivers, although the Salt Lake pattern was very different than that of San Pedro.

It is not clear that the Salt Lake toddlers and caregivers were less *able* to attend simultaneously to several events (just as the differences in the use of talk do not lead necessarily to quick conclusions about differences in the *ability* to talk); rather, the differences may reflect cultural preferences in the deployment of attention (or in the amount of talk). San Pedro parents expect their children to attend (and scold them if they do not observe—"What, have you no eyes?"[13] as reported by P. Chavajay, personal communication, December 1990), whereas Salt Lake parents are proud of their children for focusing their attention on one thing at a time (and may scold them for shifting attention, "Pay attention to what you're doing!").

The Salt Lake toddlers more frequently interrupted adult activity, per-

[13] The alert attention of the San Pedro caregivers and children also seemed to be auditory and tactile (not just visual); they responded to nearby conversation or to communication involving touch, posture, or timing without looking.

haps as a function of their caregivers' lack of attention to the toddlers' more subtle bids for attention and other ongoing activity. Salt Lake toddlers interrupted their caregivers in an average of 19% of the episodes (SD = .25), whereas San Pedro toddlers interrupted in an average of only 4% of the episodes (SD = .11), $t(18) = 1.9$, $p < .05$. If caregivers attend to one event at a time—and the "event" is not the toddler—the toddler may resort to interruption to get a caregiver's attention. (The difference is quite striking in episodes of novel object exploration during adult activity—analyzed below—as it should be if this argument is correct.)

Engaging embedded in a group versus being taught in a dyad.—The differences in attention management may relate to cultural expectations for the nature of relationships. People in San Pedro may share their attention among competing events as an aspect of frequent participation as members of groups, whereas people in Salt Lake may focus on one event at a time, functioning in a solitary fashion or dyadically even in the presence of groups. We have argued elsewhere that middle-class U.S. relationships have a dyadic prototype, with group interaction being treated as a composite of multiple dyads rather than involving action by an integrated group (Rogoff, Mistry, Göncü, & Mosier, 1991).

Our observations support the notion that the San Pedro toddlers more frequently coordinated their involvement in ways that showed them to be interacting as embedded members of a group (rather than in dyadic interactions or solitary activity). This is a matter not simply of whether a group is present but of whether the child is coordinating as a member of that group rather than functioning as a solitary actor or as a participant in single or multiple dyadic interactions. It goes beyond attention management to include coordination with different agendas and multiple activities within a group, as in the following examples:

> While 19-month-old Marina and her mother worked the jumping jack together, the mother turned Marina to face the group and directed her to watch a little boy working an identical jumping jack. As Marina's mother and an onlooker told her to hold the top string herself, Marina watched the boy working the other jumping jack, and soon skillfully suspended the jumping jack by its top string.

> José's grandmother prompted him to show us how he could dance a ceremonial dance—a little shuffling gait, turning in circles—just when his mother began to show him how the pencil box opens. José (20 months) danced a few steps while watching his mother open the box.

> As 12-month-old Chema closed things in the jar with his older sister, he managed to whistle on his toy whistle that his mother had mischievously slipped into his mouth and at the same time to watch a truck passing on the street!

The San Pedro toddlers were embedded in group interactions for at least some of the time in 53% of the episodes, but Salt Lake toddlers were embedded in group interactions in only 10% of the episodes, $t(17) = 4.1$, $p < .001$ (see Table 4).

Rather than being the exclusive, individual focus of their caregivers, the San Pedro toddlers fit into the flow of ongoing social events, with both caregivers and toddlers monitoring each other and the other social activities as they explored the novel objects. Although toddlers received attention, it was not to the exclusion of other ongoing conversations or activities; rather, they usually appeared to be smoothly integrated into the social fabric—not the recipients of toddler-directed play, special registers of speech, or exclusive attention, but already members of the group.

OBSERVATIONS OF GUIDED PARTICIPATION: DRESSING AND NOVEL OBJECT EXPLORATION DURING ADULT ACTIVITY

In order to explore whether the differences that we observed between the two communities during child-focused exploration of novel objects were a function of the particular situation, we also examined interactions in two other types of situation. The novel object episodes differ from many everyday situations in their use of novel rather than familiar objects and in the caregivers' focus on the children resulting from the interviewer's request for the caregivers to help the children work the objects. The request to get the children to work novel objects as well as the types of objects themselves were more novel for the San Pedro than for the Salt Lake caregivers and children.

Our two alternative situations involved a familiar activity (dressing) and an activity that was not focused on the child (novel object exploration during adult activity). Dressing episodes involved working a familiar object (to get the toddler's arms through the holes), with which we assumed all toddlers and their caregivers would have had experience. Episodes of novel object exploration during adult activity involved the same objects as in the novel object episodes, but interaction was not requested by the interviewer and was not the main focus of the caregiver. Instead, they involved toddler-caregiver interactions that occurred while the caregivers were focused on adult conversation and activities.

We regard the analyses of these alternative situations as exploratory since they involve at most one episode of each situation per family. All families produced a dressing episode, usually at the interviewer's request (although data were missing from one San Pedro family). Twelve of the 14 San Pedro families spontaneously produced one or more episodes of novel object exploration during adult activity, but only eight of the 14 Salt Lake families did so.

In this section, we discuss the extent to which the observations of dressing and novel object exploration during adult activity are consistent with, or require modifications of, the conclusions that we drew from the novel object episodes. The data on the primary variables for dressing and novel object exploration during adult activity appear in Tables 5–8, following the same format as for the novel objects data presented in Tables 1–4. We do not discuss each variable or use statistical analyses to examine the results of these alternative situations. The data base is too small and the number of variables too large to handle in any way other than to look for obvious modifications to the overall pattern seen in our analyses of novel object episodes.

The number of interactional moves and the extent of mutual balanced involvement in these alternative situations were similar to those in the novel object episodes in both communities.

Dressing

The pattern of community differences within the dressing episodes appears consistent with that found in the novel object episodes:

1. Salt Lake caregivers talked slightly more to the toddlers.

2. San Pedro caregivers more frequently used gesture and gaze, touch, posture, or timing cues to simplify their children's involvement, and San Pedro toddlers more frequently sought clarification with gaze. (In comparison with novel object episodes, San Pedro caregivers increased their already more frequent use of gestures and gaze, touch, posture, and timing cues in simplifying their children's involvement in dressing, and Salt Lake caregivers decreased their already less frequent use of gestures.)

3. San Pedro caregivers were also more likely to demonstrate an activity before and during the child's participation. Salt Lake caregivers used less demonstration in the dressing episodes than they had in the novel object episodes.

4. Salt Lake caregivers more frequently acted as playmates and conversed with the children as peers, and the children also conversed more often with the adults as peers.

5. Salt Lake caregivers more frequently used babytalk and gave vocabulary lessons (although with fewer vocabulary lessons than in the novel object episodes) and more frequently praised the children.

6. San Pedro caregivers were more frequently poised ready to help the child and less frequently overruled the child. Salt Lake caregivers increased the extent to which they overruled their children to 100% of the episodes,

TABLE 5

VERBAL AND NONVERBAL COMMUNICATION IN EPISODES OF DRESSING AND NOVEL OBJECT
EXPLORATION DURING ADULT ACTIVITY

	SAN PEDRO		SALT LAKE		DHOL-KI-PATTI		KEÇIÖREN	
	A	B	A	B	A	B	A	B
Number of children with an episode	13	12	14	8	14	9	14	6
Talk to child (sentences, M [SD]: 3 = 1–3; 4 = 4–9; 5 = 10+)	3.9 (1.1)	2.7 (1.3)	4.8 (.4)	2.1 (1.6)	2.5 (2.0)	.8 (1.6)	3.4 (1.6)	2.8 (1.5)
Child's talk (M [SD]: 0 = no words; 1 = 1–3 words; 2 = 4+ words; 3 = 1–3 phrases; etc.)	.7 (.9)	.9 (1.2)	.9 (.9)	2.0 (1.7)	.1 (.3)	0 (0)	.5 (.7)	1.3 (1.5)
Caregiver orients child verbally (number of children)	9	0	12	1	9	1	6	0
Caregiver orients child nonverbally (number of children)	10	0	8	0	6	2	1	0
Caregiver simplifies verbally (number of children)	12	5	12	4	8	1	10	3
Caregiver simplifies by adjustment of object or child's hands (number of children)	13	11	12	5	13	5	14	4
Caregiver simplifies by gesture (number of children)	13	5	2	1	3	3	1	0
Caregiver simplifies by gaze, touch, posture, or timing cues (number of children)	11	4	1	0	8	1	1	0
Child seeks assistance verbally (number of children)	1	4	1	3	0	0	0	1
Child seeks assistance with gestures (number of children)	0	5	2	3	2	6	0	1
Child seeks assistance with gaze, touch, posture, or timing cues (number of children)	1	6	0	1	2	3	0	0
Child seeks clarification with gaze (number of children)	7	3	1	1	[a]		[a]	

NOTE.—Values in the "A" columns represent dressing episodes, and those in the "B" columns represent novel object exploration during adult activity.

[a] This variable was dropped from analysis in these two communities (see Chap. III).

TABLE 6

EXPLANATION AND DEMONSTRATION IN EPISODES OF DRESSING AND NOVEL OBJECT
EXPLORATION DURING ADULT ACTIVITY

	SAN PEDRO		SALT LAKE		DHOL-KI-PATTI		KEÇIÖREN	
	A	B	A	B	A	B	A	B
Number of children with an episode	13	12	14	8	14	9	14	6
Extending to other situations (number of children)	0	0	3	0	0	0	3	0
Demonstration before child participates (M [SD]: 0 = none; 1 = brief; 2 = moderate; 3 = extensive) ...	1.1 (.8)	0 (0)	.1 (.4)	0 (0)	.4 (.6)	.2 (.7)	.1 (.3)	0 (0)
Demonstration during child participation (as in previous entry)	1.5 (.9)	1.4 (.9)	.6 (.6)	.9 (.8)	1.9 (.7)	1.1 (.9)	.4 (.5)	1.3 (.8)
Directing attention to process (number of children)	1	3	0	0	2	0	1	1
Turning task over to child (number of children)	1	2	1	0	0	0	0	0

NOTE.—Values in the "A" columns represent dressing episodes, and those in the "B" columns represent novel object exploration during adult activity.

making the difference between communities even more extreme. San Pedro caregivers tried to convince their children to participate in dressing, but did not force them.

7. The differences between communities in attention management that were observed in the novel object episodes were maintained in dressing, with more frequent use of simultaneous attention to competing events by both San Pedro caregivers and toddlers.

8. The San Pedro toddlers functioned as members of groups, embedded in group rather than dyadic or solo activity, to a greater extent than the Salt Lake toddlers.

Thus the results obtained in the dressing episodes support the conclusions drawn from those of the novel object episodes.

Novel Object Exploration during Adult Activity

The pattern of data in episodes of novel object exploration during adult activity further highlights some of the differences seen in the novel object and dressing episodes. It appears that the Salt Lake caregivers dropped their organizational, instructional approach to the children when engaged with other adults but that the San Pedro caregivers maintained

TABLE 7

ADULT TEACHING VERSUS SUPPORT FOR CHILD LEARNING IN EPISODES OF DRESSING AND
NOVEL OBJECT EXPLORATION DURING ADULT ACTIVITY

	SAN PEDRO		SALT LAKE		DHOL-KI-PATTI		KEÇIÖREN	
	A	B	A	B	A	B	A	B
Number of children with an episode	13	12	14	8	14	9	14	6
Caregiver acts as playmate (number of children)	0	0	7	2	2	0	4	0
Adult converses with child as peer (number of children)	2	0	10	2	5	1	9	1
Child converses with adult as peer (number of children)	1	2	6	4	2	1	6	1
Caregiver uses babytalk (number of children)	4	0	14	4	5	1	8	1
Caregiver vocabulary lesson (M [SD]: max score = 5)	.4 (.7)	0 (0)	1.4 (.7)	.8 (1.2)	.4 (.9)	.1 (.3)	.9 (1.1)	.2 (.4)
Child vocabulary lesson (M [SD]: max score = 3) ..	.1 (.3)	.2 (.4)	.1 (.4)	.1 (.4)	0 (0)	0 (0)	.2 (.4)	0 (0)
Caregiver mock excitement (number of children)	5	0	7	0	1	0	5	0
Caregiver praise (number of children)	0	0	6	0	0	0	5	0
Caregiver poised ready to help (number of children)	8	10	1	2	3	3	2	1
Caregiver overrules child (number of episodes out of number that child refused/insisted)	1/6	0/6	8/8	2/4	[a]		9/9	4/4

NOTE.—Values in the "A" columns represent dressing episodes, and those in the "B" columns represent novel object exploration during adult activity.

[a] This variable was dropped from analysis for this community (see Chap. III).

their posture toward the children of supportive and attentive assistance when engaged with other adults. These findings may relate most closely to the community differences in attention management. If the Salt Lake caregivers devote their attention to only one event at a time, it is not surprising that they cease their instructional efforts toward the children when attending to adult activity. And, if the San Pedro caregivers share their attention among several events simultaneously, with no one event inter-

TABLE 8

ATTENTION MANAGEMENT AND ENGAGEMENT EMBEDDED IN GROUP IN EPISODES OF
DRESSING AND NOVEL OBJECT EXPLORATION DURING ADULT ACTIVITY

	SAN PEDRO		SALT LAKE		DHOL-KI-PATTI		KEÇIÖREN	
	A	B	A	B	A	B	A	B
Number of children with an episode	13	12	14	8	14	9	14	6
Child attends simultaneously (M [SD]: 0 = never; 4 = overwhelming)	2.4 (1.0)	2.9 (.7)	.6 (.6)	.4 (.5)	.5 (1.1)	.6 (1.0)	a	
Child attends alternately (as in previous entry)	1.4 (1.0)	.7 (.8)	2.1 (.8)	2.6 (1.1)	1.9 (1.3)	2.4 (1.4)	a	
Child appears unaware of events (as above)	.5 (.5)	.2 (.6)	1.8 (1.0)	.8 (1.0)	.8 (1.3)	1.2 (1.1)	a	
Caregiver attends simultaneously (as above)	3.2 (.4)	3.8 (.4)	2.3 (1.4)	1.5 (1.2)	2.6 (1.6)	2.7 (1.6)	a	
Caregiver attends alternately (as above)	.4 (.5)	.5 (.5)	1.2 (1.2)	2.1 (1.1)	.7 (1.1)	1.7 (1.3)	a	
Caregiver appears unaware of events (as above)	0 (0)	.1 (.3)	.4 (.6)	1.0 (1.3)	.4 (.8)	.4 (.5)	a	
Engagement embedded in group (number of children)	9	6	3	1	3	4	4	0

NOTE.—Values in the "A" columns represent dressing episodes, and those in the "B" columns represent novel object exploration during adult activity.

[a] These variables were dropped from analysis for this community (see Chap. III).

rupting involvement with another, it is not surprising that they continue their support of their children's efforts and maintain subtle communication with their children while involved with other, adult activities.

The community difference in frequency of novel object exploration during adult activity is in itself a finding that supports our observations of differences in attention management in the two communities. In San Pedro, where caregivers commonly shared their attention among several events simultaneously, the families averaged 3.1 episodes of novel object exploration during adult activity, whereas, in Salt Lake, the families averaged only 1.4 such episodes, $t(22) = 2.5$, $p < .05$.

It is important to remember that novel object exploration during adult activity was less common overall in Salt Lake and that the data involve only eight of the 14 children. Nonetheless, some interesting patterns stand out.

1. The frequency with which the Salt Lake caregivers acted as play-mate, conversed with the child as a peer, used babytalk, gave vocabulary lessons, showed mock excitement, and praised the children decreased greatly, although they still did most of these activities more than the San Pedro caregivers. Instead of talking to the children more than San Pedro caregivers, Salt Lake caregivers averaged slightly less talking to their toddlers.

2. Nonetheless, Salt Lake toddlers spoke more while exploring a novel object during adult activity than did either San Pedro toddlers or Salt Lake toddlers themselves during the novel object or dressing episodes. This may relate to the greater frequency with which the Salt Lake toddlers interrupted their caregivers during these adult activities.

3. It seems that, when Salt Lake caregivers were involved in adult activities, the toddlers may have had to resort to strong means to get attention, whereas San Pedro toddlers received attention as a matter of course even when the caregivers were concurrently engaged with adult activities. Salt Lake toddlers interrupted during an average of 19% of the novel object episodes, two of the 14 dressing episodes, and fully five of the eight episodes of novel object exploration during adult activity. (The comparable figures for San Pedro toddlers were 4% of the novel object episodes, zero of 13 dressing episodes, and two of 12 adult activity episodes.) To give an idea of the differences in interruption by toddlers and attention by caregivers, we present contrasting events from Salt Lake and San Pedro in which toddlers sought assistance from their mothers. (Both happen not to be coded data but did involve objects brought by the researchers that were not structured by the interviewers' requests or agenda.)

An example of Salt Lake interruption was provided by 20-month-old Judy, who noticed that her sister had taken the baby doll that she had been playing with:

> As her mother chatted with the interviewer, Judy quietly murmured, "Baby, baby, baby." With no response, Judy escalated her tone and shook her head, "*Bay*-be, *bay*-be, *bay*-be. . . ." She pulled on her mother's leg, "*Bay*-bee, I *wan* it!" Her mother paid no attention to Judy and continued talking.
>
> Judy demanded, "*Bay*-bee, I *wan* it!!" over and over, occasionally looking at her sister while her mother continued talking to the adults.
>
> Finally, when her mother finished her story to the interviewer, she looked around, asking with puzzlement, "Well, where did the baby go?" It appeared that the mother really did not know that the sister had taken the doll and that Judy had been trying to get her to help get it back—she encouraged Judy to find it as if it were misplaced. Judy

complained "Mom" in a pitiful tone and waited for her mother to do something, but her mother asked curiously, "Well, where do you think the baby went?" Judy fiddled with another object, and her mother resumed talking with the interviewer.

When her sister moved away with the doll, Judy resumed her requests—"I wanna baby"—softly and persistently several times; then she looked at her mother and said with more force, "I *wan* a baby!"

Not until the sister called across the room—"I *want* it"—did the mother attend. She quit the adult conversation and engaged in an extensive child-focused episode to resolve the issue by negotiating with the sister to return the doll to Judy. Then she resumed talking with the interviewer, and Judy gave a sneaky smile to the camera operator.

This incident, full of interruptions and with the mother seemingly unaware of ongoing events, contrasts with the shared attention and smooth, unobtrusive communication without interruptions displayed during an episode involving 18-month-old Nila, from San Pedro, who needed help getting cookies from a plastic wrapper during adult activity:

During the interview, when Nila held the package up to her mother, her mother asked if she wanted a cookie, and Nila nodded yes. Her mother smiled quietly at Nila and opened the cookie package as she attended to the interviewers.

Nila attended to the interviewers too, so when her mother got the cookie out of the package, she offered it to Nila by moving her own arm, on which Nila's hand rested, so that Nila's hand touched the cookie. Nila took the cookie and ate it, then subtly requested another by gently pushing her mother's hand toward the cookies beside her on the patio. As the mother continued to attend to the interviewers she readily responded to Nila's gesture and picked up the package without looking at Nila or the package. She handed it to Nila, then glanced down at it quietly and took it back [the package was difficult for a toddler to open], and looked back at the interviewers as she took out another cookie. Once the cookie was out of the package, she took Nila's hand and moved it to the cookie that she held in her other hand, still conversing with the interviewers. She glanced down at the package only once during this unobtrusive event. The interaction with Nila did not disrupt the flow of the interview in the least.

4. San Pedro toddlers were at least as interested as those in Salt Lake in engaging with their caregivers, as evidenced by the greater frequency with which they requested assistance (especially via gaze, touch, posture, or timing cues as in the example of Nila) and with which they acted as a part of the group (as in Nila's attention to the group's main activity, the inter-

view). It appears that the San Pedro toddlers could request assistance in their normal fashion whereas the Salt Lake toddlers had to interrupt forcefully to get their caregivers' attention.

5. San Pedro caregivers were more likely to maintain a readiness to help the child than Salt Lake caregivers and remained less likely to overrule the child's refusal or insistence.

6. The differences between communities in attention management were maintained, with greater simultaneity of attention and less unawareness of competing events in San Pedro by both caregivers and toddlers, although in these episodes all the families were more likely to share their attention among competing events.

These points are well illustrated by returning to Sandy and Juan, whose interactions with their mothers with the jar and peewee were described in the novel object section. Sandy's episode was one of the longest and most interactive of the Salt Lake episodes of novel object exploration during adult activity. During adult conversation, 21-month-old Sandy tried to involve his mother with the jar and peewee again, in an excellent example of alternating attention by the mother:

> As his mother and the interviewer talked, Sandy tried to reach the jar (with a round knob on the lid). He pointed and said, "Want ball," reached and said, "Ball," then grunted, saying, "Ball, ball," and finally stretched and barely reached it. His mother eventually saw what he was doing and stopped talking with the interviewer.
>
> She proceeded to interact with Sandy exclusively, picking up the jar, "What is that? You want that back?" They engaged in an exclusive interaction that was long enough to suspend the coding of adult activity. Now, as she focused on Sandy, the mother interacted with him as she did during the earlier novel object episode, with conversational peer questions, vocabulary lessons, and her full attention: "What's in there? . . . The baby?" When Sandy put the peewee in the jar and closed the lid, she prompted, "Say bye-bye."
>
> Sandy became distracted as the camera operator moved the camera, and he too exhibited a focus on one event at a time, as he turned around and watched the camera operator.
>
> At this, the adult conversation resumed. Then Sandy played with the jar and talked to his mother, who glanced at him from time to time but did not respond or stop talking with the interviewer.
>
> Sandy alternated his attention between the camera operator and his play. His mother finished talking with the interviewer and looked down to see Sandy playing with the Play-Doh. "Oh, it's a pancake!" she chirped, "Wanna put it in there?" moving into a child-focused moment of attention and shared action.
>
> The interviewer asked a question, and the mother resumed attending to the interviewer. Sandy continued to play, turning his atten-

tion from time to time to smile at the camera operator. During subsequent interaction, Sandy's mother occasionally monitored him or alternated attention to him momentarily as she conversed with the interviewer, but she seemed not to notice when Sandy offered her a piece of cookie.

Although the interaction between Sandy and his mother is one of the most extensive episodes from Salt Lake of novel object exploration during adult activity, it contrasts with the interaction described earlier between 20-month-old Juan and his mother with the jar. In fact, Juan and his mother's interaction involved both ongoing adult activity and child-focused activity at the same time in such a way that, if a coder focused on the interaction with the child, the mother's ready help with working the object appeared to be uninterrupted by her involvement in adult conversation but, if the coder focused on the mother's involvement in adult activity, it too appeared uninterrupted by her interactions with the child. This was characteristic of the whole of Juan and his family's session, and many of the other San Pedro families exhibited a number of extensive episodes of this sort.

It appears that the child-focused nature of the novel object episodes differed in some systematic ways from the exploration during adult activity episodes for the Salt Lake families, with the instructional organization by the Salt Lake caregivers being limited to times during which they focused on the children. By contrast, the sensitive assistance approach of the San Pedro caregivers occurred both when the children were the caregivers' exclusive focus and when the caregivers were concurrently focused on adult activities.

In fact, there was evidence in some of the San Pedro children's reactions to the novel object situation that they may have been uncomfortable with the undivided adult attention that that situation entailed. In several cases, the San Pedro toddlers refused the novel objects when the children were the focus of attention, but subtly picked the objects up with interest and skillfully explored them with their caregivers' assistance once the adults moved to adult conversation.

VARIATIONS WITHIN SAN PEDRO
ASSOCIATED WITH MOTHERS' SCHOOLING

Variation in mothers' schooling in San Pedro gave us the possibility of examining differences that may be related to exposure to this Western institution. Although the sample size was only 14, we had the impression that the five San Pedro mothers who had more schooling (sixth to ninth grade) talked with their children in ways that were more similar to those of

Salt Lake mothers but that their means of attention management did not appear to differ from that of the nine mothers with less schooling (none to third grade; there were no mothers with fourth- or fifth-grade schooling). It seemed that, with greater experience of school, the mothers would use one or another aspect of school talk with their toddlers (although this did not appear to come as a package—one mother would treat her child as a conversational peer, another would act as a playmate, and so on). Our impressions were supported by our coded data, which we used to examine the relations between mothers' schooling and the primary maternal variables that showed differences between San Pedro and Salt Lake, using the novel object data.

The amount of talk to the child and of extending to other situations was generally higher among all the mothers with more than a sixth-grade education than among those with a third-grade education or less (r's = .47 and .59, respectively; both p's < .05). The five mothers with more than a sixth-grade education were the only ones who exhibited the following characteristics, and those five were split between those who exhibited them a great deal and those who did not do so at all. Three of the five acted as a playmate in one or two episodes, whereas only one of the nine mothers with less schooling did so (r = .50, p < .05). Three of the five conversed with the child as a peer in most of the episodes, whereas the other two did not do so at all; eight of the nine mothers with less schooling never conversed with the child as a peer, and one did only once (r = .54, p < .05). Use of babytalk, caregiver's vocabulary lessons, and use of mock excitement followed the same pattern: the only San Pedro mothers who consistently exhibited these practices were a few of those with more schooling; others among the five, along with mothers with less schooling, rarely or never engaged in these practices (r's = .41, .43, .22, N.S., respectively). Praise was so seldom used by any of the San Pedro caregivers that no differences between mothers with more or less schooling emerged. As we had thought, there was no relation between the extent of the mother's schooling and her means of attention management (r's for caregiver attending simultaneously, alternating, or appearing unaware were −.05, −.15, and −.12, respectively).

It appears that the experience of schooling provided particular discourse practices that are being adopted bit by bit in San Pedro (amount of talk, explanation, and language lessons; acting as a peer with the child in conversation and play; and taking responsibility for motivating the child) but that the pattern of attention management may be a more resilient cultural pattern. It is consequently of special interest to examine the ways in which mothers in Keçiören managed their attention, coming as they do from a community with traditional roots but greater exposure to schooling. These mothers may speak to their children like the Salt Lake caregivers, but, like the more schooled San Pedro mothers, they may share their attention among competing events more than the Salt Lake mothers.

SUMMARY

The pattern of differences between San Pedro and Salt Lake is consistent with the idea that San Pedro toddlers have greater opportunity to observe adult activity, are more likely to attend to several events simultaneously (as are their caregivers), and are more likely to take the lead in solving problems, with their caregivers demonstrating the processes and responsively assisting the children when they request assistance. The communication between San Pedro caregivers and children relied more heavily on nonverbal means of communication than did that between the Salt Lake caregivers and children.

The Salt Lake toddlers and caregivers were more likely to attend to one event at a time. When the Salt Lake caregivers were attending to the toddlers, they organized the toddlers' motivation through mock excitement and praise, sometimes overruling the toddlers' direction, and they provided lessons in language use and extended the situation at hand to other contexts. Rather than supporting the children's participation in adult activities and integration in the group, Salt Lake caregivers interacted with their toddlers dyadically as peers on a child level, with caregivers acting as toddlers' peers in play and with caregivers and toddlers engaging in conversation as peers when they attended to each other; when their attention was focused on a competing event, however, such interaction dropped off dramatically.

These observations support our contrast between patterns of guided participation involving, on the one hand, children taking primary responsibility for their own learning with the support of their caregivers and, on the other, caregivers taking heavy responsibility for the children's learning by organizing lessons.

V. GUIDED PARTICIPATION IN DHOL-KI-PATTI

Jayanthi Mistry

This chapter focuses on describing guided participation between caregivers and toddlers in Dhol-Ki-Patti. As in the previous chapter, the community is described first, with background information provided on the 14 families that constitute the sample. The description of the community is based on the researcher's general familiarity with the area (Udaipur and its surrounding villages), conversations with friends and relatives who are involved in development work in the region, documents and publications about this tribal region and about the village itself, and conversations with the researcher's assistant (a teacher in the village primary school) and the families in our sample. The information on the families comes from the interviews that we conducted during the visits.

BACKGROUND OF THE COMMUNITY AND FAMILIES IN DHOL-KI-PATTI

The sample was drawn from a rural roadside tribal village named Dhol-Ki-Patti that is located 10 km from Udaipur, a city in the state of Rajasthan. Owing to its proximity to a city, Dhol-Ki-Patti is exposed to urban influences. Many of the men work as daily paid laborers in the city or neighboring villages, thus having more contact with nontribal communities than is generally typical for tribal villages. Women are responsible for child care and household activities and often for helping with farm work as well. Occasionally, women also go to the city to work as daily paid laborers, especially during seasons of light farm work.

Most of the fathers (11 of 13) in the Dhol-Ki-Patti sample were involved in agriculture, either as agricultural laborers or as farmers on their own small holdings. One father was a semiskilled worker, and another owned a small store. Only two mothers were primarily housewives; most of them (10 of 14) worked on the family's land in addition to carrying out household tasks. Two of the mothers worked as factory workers or hired laborers near the city.

Dhol-Ki-Patti is situated within the area where most of Rajasthan's tribal villages are concentrated. Like other tribal villages, this one is relatively homogeneous with respect to religion, caste, occupation, and general income level. All residents of the village belong to the Gameti clan of the Adivasi tribe of Rajasthan. All families spoke the local Rajasthani dialect and practiced tribal religion, characterized by a common base of man-supernatural interaction (Maim, 1978), with influences from animistic religions and Hinduism.

The Adivasis have been described as "children of the forest" (Government of Rajasthan, 1988, p. 5) because they were previously a community of nomadic "gatherers" who lived off the products of the forest but who have now been forced to turn to agricultural labor as deforestation and other factors have led to the need for settlement. This has caused many changes in their way of life. Some authors have argued that there has been an erosion of some of the unique strengths of traditional tribal people (Doshi, 1978; Mann, 1988), such as egalitarianism between the genders, the collective nature of life in the communities, and the role of work and occupation and its implication for families.

Dhol-Ki-Patti residents practice subsistence agriculture on small land-holdings (less than 3 acres) and generally need to work as agricultural laborers or construction workers during the agricultural off season. Families generally have only enough resources (financial, material, food) to get by. In spite of this, it seems inappropriate to use words like "poverty" to describe their economic conditions because indicators such as average income level do not make sense in a subsistence economy. Moreover, families generally own some land, however little, and own their own homes, however small—so they would not call themselves "poor." Nonetheless, in comparison with the other three communities we studied, the living conditions of the Dhol-Ki-Patti sample were more marginal.

The village has a government primary school but does not have any medical facilities (the nearest one is 5 km away), a market, or a post office. It is supplied with electricity for agricultural irrigation only. The village is dependent on wells for its water supply, and there is no electricity for domestic use. Families grow their own food and exist primarily on the staples maize and wheat.

There was evidence of malnutrition among some of the children in our sample, but it is not clear if this was a function of insufficient food or of different notions about what constitutes an adequate diet for babies. For example, the toddlers in our sample were not given vegetables, and, when asked about this, caregivers often replied that vegetables cause diarrhea in young children. Most of the toddlers (nine of 14) were still nursing.

There are about 100 households in Dhol-Ki-Patti, spread out in clusters of 10–20 households. This is characteristic of tribal villages, as families prefer to build their homes next to their fields. The extended family living within a compound are all paternal kin. In fact, for all but one of the families, relatives within the village were paternal kin, as men typically marry women from other villages, and women move to the husband's village on marriage. For one family, this is the mother's village because her husband left her and she returned to the village of her birth to live near her parents.

All families live in one of a set of one-room mud houses constructed around a central courtyard. Members of the extended family live in the adjacent houses. Nuclear units consisting of parents and children live in each one-room home and cook and eat separately from the extended family. The units share a common bathing/washing area.

The families in our sample contained one to seven children (mean = 2.8). The target children were the youngest in all but two families; in addition, one mother was pregnant at the time of the visits. Four mothers reported the death of a previous child. All but one family had both mother and father living in the same household—one mother was a single parent who lived with her parents. Exact ages are not kept track of; however, mothers' and fathers' ages are usually similar.

The collective nature of life in tribal communities was reflected in several ways in our Dhol-Ki-Patti sample. For example, when answering interview questions about the composition of the family and the proximity of relatives, caregivers often used the terms "family" and "relatives" more inclusively than did the interviewer. Members of the extended family were considered "family" even though they were not considered part of the same household because they did not share the same hearth. Neighbors are often related, and, if not, they have been living next to each other for generations and behave like relatives through the sense of community and belonging (Mistry, Göncü, & Rogoff, 1988).

Age Segregation

In Dhol-Ki-Patti, the collective nature of life ensures that children have many opportunities to participate in the social life of the community. Children are not segregated from adults, and there is a focus on people and their activities rather than on objects. Even the child-care network is collective, with responsibility for caregiving diffused throughout a neighborhood group. Babies are usually surrounded by neighbors of many ages, kin and nonkin, adults and children, who take responsibility for them when the mother is away in the fields or busy with chores. Only two Dhol-Ki-Patti mothers reported themselves as the sole caregiver; most (nine out of 14) named other children as major helpers with child care, and three reported getting assistance from other adult relatives.

Babies were in social contact most of the time, playing with neighbor children during the day and sleeping with family members at night. All but one of the toddlers in the Dhol-Ki-Patti sample slept in the same bed with the mother—one child slept in the same room but with siblings. The toddlers' waking hours were spent with easy access to adults as they work in fields or in factories, complete chores or household tasks, and engage in leisure, social, or religious activities. Even when groups of 10–15 children took care of each other in common areas (e.g., open courtyards or spaces between clusters of homes), they were close to their parents, who were working in the fields nearby. From the beginning, children are included in ongoing adult activities as part of a close-knit, fluid community.

Goals of Development

In Dhol-Ki-Patti, child-rearing goals are not something that people reflect on or express opinions about. When asked what they hoped or wanted for their children's future, most caregivers (10 of 14) shrugged off the question or indicated that the future was in the hands of fate. Such answers reflected an attitude of being open to whatever was written in the child's destiny, without any tone of the pessimism or futility that is usually associated with such beliefs. Caregivers see their role as taking care of and preparing the child for adulthood, which they assume will be similar to their own lives as adults. Perhaps caregivers do not need to reflect on child-rearing goals because children learn to become members of the community through gradual participation in adult activities and taking responsibility for their own learning. When Dhol-Ki-Patti caregivers were asked whether and how they taught their toddlers appropriate behavior or etiquette, eight of them either shrugged off the question or said that children "just learn," while six gave specific examples of how their children have started imitating adult actions and behaviors or have started participating in festivals or worship rituals (such as bowing heads before religious deities).

Formal schooling is not a high priority for most families. According to the schoolteacher, most children go through about 2–4 years of schooling and begin to drop out at the age of 7–9 years to help out at home or in the field. Teachers consider it an achievement if even five or six children in the village complete elementary school and go on to the intermediate school in a nearby village. Information on number of years of schooling was hard to obtain for the Dhol-Ki-Patti parents. Often, they could not specify a definite number of years, perhaps because of intermittent attendance. However, from the schoolteachers' and caregivers' responses, we were able to determine that two fathers had completed high school while the others had less than a few years of schooling and were not literate. All the mothers had less than one or two years of schooling.

Child-rearing practices and milestones reached by the toddlers in Dhol-Ki-Patti were quite different than those reported for Salt Lake toddlers. Most of the toddlers (nine of 14) were toilet trained, three were in the process, and two (the youngest ones in our sample) had not yet begun. Seven toddlers were walking steadily, two were in the process of learning, and five had not yet begun. Most of the toddlers had not begun to talk yet (nine of 14), and five were using fewer than five or six words.

Orientation toward Participating in the Study

The senior teacher of the village elementary school served as the primary informant and as the researcher's assistant for collecting data. Although the teacher had a long-standing personal relationship with most of the families, her higher social status (through her role as teacher), along with the fact that the researcher was a "visitor" from the city, may have set up a more "formal" situation for the visits than obtained in the other communities considered in this study.

The observations should consequently be seen as representing "public behavior." However, "public behavior" does not imply that the families were "putting on" behavior that was not typical. Since much of life in rural Indian settings is lived outdoors (in open courtyards), most behavior is "public" in the sense of being visible to all who are around. However, because of our perceived higher status, there may have been an element of reserve and deference among the families, who participated out of a desire to accommodate the schoolteacher, who requested their participation on the researcher's behalf.

The "object-oriented interaction between adults and children" of the novel objects episodes may not be as typical an activity for the Dhol-Ki-Patti families as for those in Salt Lake and Keçiören. While the caregivers were instructed to engage with the child in handling or exploring the objects, they may have perceived it as a "play" situation because some of the novel objects were toys. The usual context for adult-child interaction (other than caretaking) is one of expressing affection (*laad*) and of enjoying children. Such mutual engagement between adult and child is interactive, with partners' attention and playful actions focused on each other, but it does not involve joint attention to toys or objects. In fact, caregivers treat toys as something to be used to keep a toddler busy while the adults go about their chores.

Adult caregivers, especially mothers, seemed uninterested during some of the novel object interactions. Sometimes, when we repeated the instructions to help the toddler explore or handle the objects, adult caregivers became uncomfortable and embarrassed as if they were being asked to do something unusual. For example, when the researcher's assistant repeated the instruction to one of the mothers to "get" her child to handle the novel object, the mother became confused and hesitant. In another case, the mother sat with her toddler in the open courtyard during the initial interview questions, but, when the novel objects were brought out, she took that as a cue that now it was all right for her to leave the immediate vicinity of the toddler and go about her chores in the courtyard. When we called her back and specifically asked her to stay and help get the child engaged with the objects, she complied with our request in an embarrassed, self-conscious manner.

Two of the novel objects (the embroidery hoops and the pencil box) were dropped from the analysis in Dhol-Ki-Patti because these elicited only one to three interactive moves in many dyads. If the toddlers did not demonstrate interest in these objects, the caregivers did not try to "get" them interested. This acceptance of the child's lack of interest reflects an expectation that object play is within children's realm and that it is not caregivers' business to direct play. The remaining novel objects elicited enough interactive moves and interest to enable confident analysis of patterns of behavior in object-oriented interaction.

In the following sections, the pattern of results for Dhol-Ki-Patti is contrasted with that for the Salt Lake data so as to examine differences between communities that may reflect differences in patterns of segregation between adult and child worlds, with the San Pedro data being used for examination of similarities in pattern.

OBSERVATIONS OF GUIDED PARTICIPATION: NOVEL OBJECTS

Preliminary Analyses

The Dhol-Ki-Patti toddlers were no different from those in Salt Lake in the number of interactional moves they made during the novel object situation, once the two novel objects that did not elicit interaction were dropped from analysis (leaving an average of 3.1 objects per child; range = 2–4). Toddlers averaged 10–20 moves during the novel object interactions, a number similar to that obtained in the Salt Lake sample (difference N.S.).

As in the other communities, the Dhol-Ki-Patti toddlers usually had at least one adult partner—typically the mother, although in two cases fathers were the only adult partners. In 24% of the novel object episodes, toddlers had child partners as well as adult partners (significantly more than the Salt Lake toddlers, who had child partners in 3% of the episodes, $t = 2.1$, $p <$ .05). This pattern of having both adult and child partners was similar to that observed in San Pedro. In a few cases, only child partners were involved in the Dhol-Ki-Patti episodes (although an adult was present), unlike either the San Pedro or the Salt Lake sample. The fact that neighbors and kin were always around during these sessions and comfortably participated in them (offering suggestions or advice to caregivers, answering questions on their behalf, and so on) reflected the familiar involvement of neighbors and kin in each other's lives (Mistry, Rogoff, & Göncü, 1987).

Descriptive Data and Graphs

Means and standard deviations involved in the similarities and differences between communities that are described in the following sections appear in Tables 1–4. We present graphs accompanying the key discussions of differences that also show the means (marked by a black square; for an example, see Fig. 12). The graphs are intended to make the patterns easier

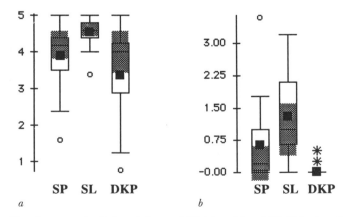

FIG. 12.—Amount of talk by adults to child (a) and by child (b) in San Pedro (SP), Salt Lake (SL), and Dhol-Ki-Patti (DKP). For an explanation of the symbols, see the text. Rating scale of amount of talk to child: (3) = 1–3 sentences; 4 = 4–9 sentences; 5 = 10+ sentences. Rating scale of amount of talk by child: 0 = no words; 1 = 1–3 words; 2 = 4+ words; 3 = 1–3 phrases; 4 = 4+ phrases.

to follow and are a key tool used by the research team to understand the patterns. (We used such graphs for every variable.)

The graphs show box plots from the data analysis program that we used (DataDesk). In addition to indicating mean values (which we have added to the DataDesk plots), the box plots in the graphs provide a great deal of information on the distribution of individual families: the median (the horizontal line across the box), the middle half of the data between the 25th and the 75th percentiles (the outlined central box), the range of the main body of the data (the whiskers extending above and below the box), and outliers (plotted with circles or, if extreme, with an asterisk). The box plots also show the 95% confidence intervals for comparing medians (the shaded area); these are constructed so that, if the shaded areas of two communities do not overlap, the corresponding medians are discernibly different at approximately the 5% significance level. We used the confidence interval information to inform our comparisons of means, reported in the sections below using t tests.

Cultural Similarities in Guided Participation

Creating Bridges

Data on the extent of mutual engagement could not be analyzed owing to the low reliability of codings on this variable. However, as in other communities, Dhol-Ki-Patti caregivers provided bridging by orienting the toddlers to the activity. Caregivers provided orientation in 91% of the episodes, an extent that did not differ from Salt Lake (where it also occurred in 91% of the episodes).

Structuring

As in the other communities, caregivers and toddlers jointly structured their involvement in the interactions. Most Dhol-Ki-Patti caregivers (73%) used one or another means of simplifying the task for the toddlers (not significantly different from the 87% of Salt Lake caregivers or the 93% of San Pedro caregivers who did so).

Most toddlers also used one or another means to structure their involvement in the activity. Similar to the Salt Lake and the San Pedro samples, in 24% of the episodes the Dhol-Ki-Patti toddlers introduced information or structure to the activity (compared to 29% of episodes in Salt Lake, N.S.); in 80% of the episodes they sought involvement (compared to 79% in Salt Lake, N.S.); and in 38% they sought assistance (compared to 33% in Salt Lake, N.S.).

Cultural Variation in Guided Participation

Means of Communication and Instruction

Verbal and nonverbal communication.—As in San Pedro, in Dhol-Ki-Patti caregivers and toddlers were more likely than those in Salt Lake to use nonverbal means of communicating and less likely to use verbal means (see Table 1 and Figure 12 above). Dhol-Ki-Patti caregivers averaged about three sentences of speech directed to the toddlers, while Salt Lake caregivers averaged four to nine sentences, $t(15) = 3.0$, $p < .01$. Similarly, Dhol-Ki-Patti toddlers averaged less than one word per episode, whereas Salt Lake toddlers averaged one to three words, $t(13) = 4.8$, $p < .001$.

Like their San Pedro counterparts, Dhol-Ki-Patti caregivers and toddlers used a variety of subtle nonverbal means of communicating while they structured and guided each other's involvement in the novel object episodes (see Fig. 13). Although Dhol-Ki-Patti caregivers provided less verbal simplification than did the Salt Lake caregivers (45% of episodes compared to 69%, respectively, $t[22] = 2.0$, $p < .05$), most of them simplified the toddlers' involvement by adjusting the objects or guiding the child's hand. There were no differences between Dhol-Ki-Patti and Salt Lake caregivers in their use of adjustment to simplify the task for the toddler, consistent with the lack of differences between San Pedro and Salt Lake. Unlike the findings from San Pedro, however, Dhol-Ki-Patti caregivers did not differ from those in Salt Lake in the use of gestures. This may be because Dhol-Ki-Patti caregivers were more likely to use nonconventional movements (such as a peculiar head movement or facial/eye expression) to convey a message rather than conventional gestures. Such nonconventional means would be

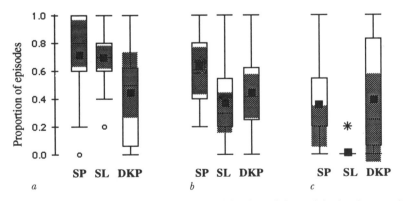

Fig. 13.—Proportion of episodes with simplification of the activity by the caregiver through means of verbal statements (*a*), gestures (*b*), or gaze, touch, posture, or timing cues (*c*) in San Pedro (SP), Salt Lake (SL), and Dhol-Ki-Patti (DKP). For an explanation of the symbols, see the text.

included in the greater frequency with which Dhol-Ki-Patti caregivers used subtle nonverbal means such as gaze, touch, posture, or timing cues to guide the toddlers. Communicative gaze, touch, posture, and timing cues that simplified the child's involvement in working the objects—almost nonexistent in the Salt Lake sample—were used in 40% of the Dhol-Ki-Patti episodes, $t(13) = 3.5, p < .01$. Like caregivers in San Pedro, those in Dhol-Ki-Patti used a more complex set of nonverbal communication means than the Salt Lake caregivers.

In the following example, a father first got an 18-month-old's attention so as to offer him the jar and then guided him in using the jar in many subtle, nonverbal ways (note that father and child did not say a single word to each other). At the same time, the father carried on a conversation with the researcher's assistant (see Fig. 14):

When the father picked up the jar with the ring inside and shook it (to make the ring rattle) to get Ramu's attention, Ramu moved closer to watch.

Fig. 14.—A Dhol-Ki-Patti father sits on his haunches demonstrating the jar as he simultaneously answers a question from the interviewer. Note that his face is turned toward the interviewer while his actions are directed toward and have captured the attention of little Ramu.

111

As the father answered a question from the researcher's assistant, he drew Ramu's attention to the ring inside the jar and demonstrated the series of actions that could be performed with the jar, by opening the lid, rattling the ring inside briefly, then closing the lid again. He did this as he held the jar out to Ramu, making sure it was in his line of vision and holding it out in an offer.

When Ramu reached for the jar, his father gave it to him and watched as Ramu began to examine the jar while he simultaneously continued his response to questions he was being asked.

Ramu took the lid off the jar, took the ring out, and triumphantly showed it to his father, holding it up to his line of vision and smiling happily.

Father nodded, acknowledging what Ramu had accomplished. Then, with a quick movement of his eyes together with a sideways nod, he prompted Ramu to put the ring inside the jar again.

Like their caregivers, Dhol-Ki-Patti toddlers also used less verbal and more subtle nonverbal means than did their Salt Lake counterparts (see Fig. 15). Although Salt Lake toddlers were more likely than the Dhol-Ki-Patti toddlers to use verbal means to seek assistance, $t(13) = 2.4$, $p < .05$, Dhol-Ki-Patti toddlers (like their San Pedro counterparts) were more likely to use gaze, touch, posture, or timing cues. They used such cues in 17% of the episodes, while Salt Lake toddlers rarely did so, $t(13) = 1.8$, $p < .05$. There were no differences between the two groups of toddlers in the use of more conventional gestures.

Explanation and demonstration.—There were no differences between the two groups of caregivers on our variable *extending to other situations* (state-

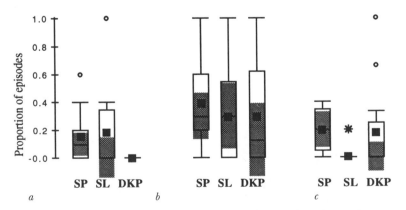

FIG. 15.—Proportion of episodes in which the toddler sought assistance by means of verbal requests (*a*), gestures (*b*), or gaze, touch, posture, or timing cues (*c*) in San Pedro (SP), Salt Lake (SL), and Dhol-Ki-Patti (DKP). For an explanation of the symbols, see the text.

ments that drew links with similar objects or situations, e.g., referring to the embroidery hoops as "bangles"). This differed from the pattern of differences between Salt Lake and San Pedro caregivers (see Table 2 above and Fig. 16). Unlike the San Pedro caregivers, the Dhol-Ki-Patti caregivers provided extension to other situations almost as much as did the Salt Lake caregivers (31% of the episodes compared to 47% of the episodes, respectively, N.S.). Most of these statements were elicited by the jumping jack, with caregivers commenting on the "dancing" action of the object. For example, one caregiver suggested that the child should "make it dance" as she tried to help the child pull on the lower string to elicit the jumping action.

Unlike the difference found between San Pedro and Salt Lake, Dhol-Ki-Patti caregivers did not use more demonstration than the Salt Lake caregivers, either before or during the child's participation in the activity (see Fig. 16). This may have been because of the Dhol-Ki-Patti caregivers' attitude that object play is in children's realm of activity and that it is not their business to manage it beyond providing brief instruction and demonstration and then turning the task over to the child. Dhol-Ki-Patti caregivers were more likely to turn the task over to the child than were the Salt Lake caregivers (in 67% vs. 16% of the episodes, respectively, $t[21] = 4.6$, $p < .0001$). The fact that Dhol-Ki-Patti caregivers (unlike those in San Pedro) did not direct toddlers' attention to important steps significantly more often than Salt Lake caregivers also suggests that the Dhol-Ki-Patti caregivers regarded their role with the objects as less instructional than did the San Pedro caregivers. The Dhol-Ki-Patti caregivers did provide extending comments (e.g., interpreting the jumping jack's actions as "dancing"), but these seem not to be deliberately instructional in the way that extensive demonstrations or detailed verbal instructions are.

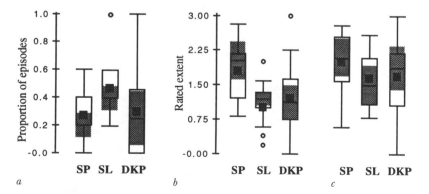

FIG. 16.—The extent to which caregivers extended the activity to other situations (*a*) and provided demonstration before (*b*) or during (*c*) children's participation in the activity in San Pedro (SP), Salt Lake (SL), and Dhol-Ki-Patti (DKP). For an explanation of the symbols, see the text.

An example of 18-month-old Roopa's mother helping her with the jumping jack illustrates the mother's efforts to turn the task over to her daughter while remaining ready to help when necessary (see Fig. 17):

> Roopa was not holding the top and bottom strings taut enough to cause the jumping jack to jump, so her mother took Roopa's hand in her own, grasped the bottom string with both hands, and pulled on the string twice, saying, "Pull here, pull here," as she demonstrated. She then released her hold of Roopa's hand to enable Roopa to do it on her own.
>
> But the jumping jack fell to the ground because Roopa was not holding it tight. The mother, quick to help, lifted the jumping jack as Roopa reached for it. Twice again, she pulled on the bottom string with her left hand, repeating, "Pull it here." Then she released her hold, letting Roopa take the object. She held her hands close to (but not touching) Roopa's, ready to help if necessary.

Adult-Child Roles in Teaching and Learning

Findings discussed in this section center around the issue of whether the child or the adult takes the responsibility for learning. As Dhol-Ki-Patti

FIG. 17.—This Dhol-Ki-Patti mother turns the jumping jack over to her daughter, Roopa, after demonstrating how to work it. Note how the mother's hand is poised ready to help.

is a community in which children are embedded in the adult world and have many opportunities to observe and be involved in adult activities, we expected that the pattern of findings would reflect the fact that it is the children who have the responsibility for learning.

Status equals in object play.—Because object-oriented play is not a typical focus for adult-child interaction but rather an activity in which children engage on their own or with other children, adults take the role of facilitating the child's play rather than engaging in it jointly. Dhol-Ki-Patti caregivers were less likely than Salt Lake caregivers to act as playmates—they did so in only 24% of the episodes, compared to 48% of the episodes in Salt Lake, $t(25) = 1.8$, $p < .05$ (see Table 3 above and Fig. 18).

Although Dhol-Ki-Patti caregivers seldom reported themselves as their child's play partners (reporting that siblings and other children typically play with the toddler), they did engage in some kinds of play (tickling, cooing, and peek-a-boo) to "express affection" and enjoy their toddlers. They also occasionally behaved as "playmates" when the play did not involve objects, as in the following example:

> When Gopi's mother tried to get him to dance for our benefit, he shook his head, refusing. Mother imitated his head shaking in a teasing way, as she playfully prevented him from climbing into her lap.
>
> Gopi imitated his mother's head shaking and grabbed the edge of her sari (draped over her head) and playfully pulled it down so that it covered her face.
>
> The mother, in turn, playfully pulled the sari edge back over her head to uncover her face with a big grin at Gopi, in a nonverbal game of "peek-a-boo."

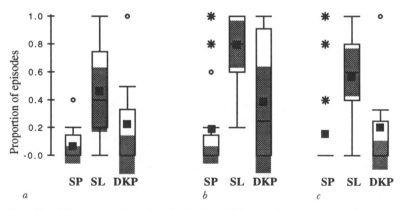

FIG. 18.—The proportion of episodes in which caregivers acted as playmates (*a*), adults conversed with child as peer (*b*), and child conversed with adults as peer (*c*) in San Pedro (SP), Salt Lake (SL), and Dhol-Ki-Patti (DKP). For an explanation of the symbols, see the text.

Adults teaching versus supporting children learning.—Unlike the Salt Lake caregivers (but like those in San Pedro), Dhol-Ki-Patti caregivers did not place themselves on the child's level by playing and conversing with the children as peers, and they did not attempt to motivate or organize their learning. Rather, they maintained availability to assist when necessary while primarily allowing the child to explore or work the object independently. These characteristics are consistent with the notion that Dhol-Ki-Patti children are responsible for their own learning.

Although Dhol-Ki-Patti toddlers and caregivers acted reciprocally with each other, they did not often take on a peer conversational role with each other (see Table 3 above and Fig. 18). Dhol-Ki-Patti caregivers less frequently interacted with toddlers as conversational peers, asking their opinions or providing openings for dialogic exchanges in only 39% of the episodes, compared with 79% in Salt Lake, $t(20) = 3.0$, $p < .01$. Similarly, Dhol-Ki-Patti toddlers took on a peer conversational role in only 20% of the episodes, compared to 57% in Salt Lake, $t(25) = 3.0$, $p < .05$.

Dhol-Ki-Patti caregivers also did not provide language lessons to their toddlers to the extent that the Salt Lake caregivers did (see Table 3 above and Fig. 19). Dhol-Ki-Patti caregivers used marked babytalk intonations in their speech to toddlers in only a third of the episodes; Salt Lake caregivers did so in almost all episodes, $t(15) = 4.1$, $p = .001$. Dhol-Ki-Patti caregivers rarely provided vocabulary lessons by labeling objects, expanding children's speech, providing running commentaries, or playing language games—they averaged less than one kind of vocabulary lesson per episode, whereas Salt Lake caregivers averaged two, $t(25) = 4.8$, $p < .0001$. The relative frequency of each type of vocabulary lesson in the Dhol-Ki-Patti and Salt Lake samples, respectively, was as follows: caregivers labeled objects in 2% versus

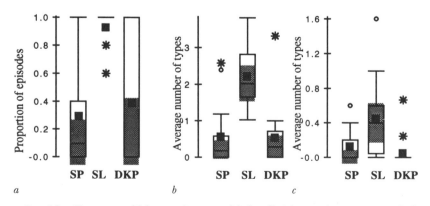

FIG. 19.—Extent to which caregivers used babytalk (*a*), caregivers gave vocabulary lessons (*b*), and child engaged in vocabulary lesson (*c*) in San Pedro (SP), Salt Lake (SL), and Dhol-Ki-Patti (DKP). For an explanation of the symbols, see the text.

50% of the episodes, requested labels in 10% versus 31%, provided running commentary on events in 29% versus 70%, expanded child speech in 5% versus 44%, and engaged in language games in 10% versus 20%.

Similarly, Dhol-Ki-Patti toddlers were less likely than Salt Lake toddlers to participate in language lessons, $t(17) = 2.9, p < .01$.

Dhol-Ki-Patti caregivers seldom attempted to organize instruction for their toddlers (see Fig. 20). They used mock excitement to motivate in only 32% of the episodes, while Salt Lake caregivers did so much more often (in 74% of the episodes), $t(23) = 3.2, p = .01$. Salt Lake caregivers were also more likely to use praise to reward and maintain the children's involvement than were Dhol-Ki-Patti caregivers (44% vs. 5%, respectively, $t[20] = 4.2$, $p < .001$).

Consistent with allowing the child to set the goals and agenda of object play while being available and responsive to even quite subtle cues for assistance, Dhol-Ki-Patti caregivers were more likely than their Salt Lake counterparts to be poised in readiness to assist (in 65% as compared to 23% of episodes, respectively, $t[21] = 3.5, p = .01$; see Fig. 20). They were ready to help according to the toddler's need rather than organizing instruction according to their own plans (see Fig. 17 above).

The notion that object play belongs in the child's domain of activity was reflected in findings that the Dhol-Ki-Patti toddlers were about twice as likely to refuse or insist than were the Salt Lake toddlers (60% of episodes compared to 33%, respectively, $t[25] = 2.4, p = .05$). Owing to the marginal reliability of codings, we could not compare caregivers' tendency to overrule the toddler's insistence, although it appeared to be about half as frequent as in Salt Lake.

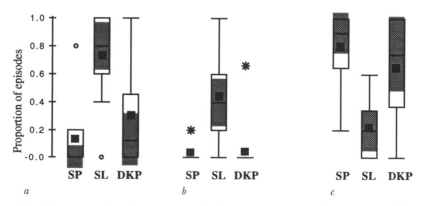

FIG. 20.—Proportion of episodes in which caregivers attempted to motivate children with mock excitement (*a*) or praise (*b*) and were poised ready to help children (*c*) in San Pedro (SP), Salt Lake (SL), and Dhol-Ki-Patti (DKP). For an explanation of the symbols, see the text.

Learning through Observation

Management of attention.—As noted previously, we expect that, in cultural communities in which learning occurs through participation in adult activity, children may become keen observers, sharing their attention among several ongoing events. Dhol-Ki-Patti toddlers were more likely than Salt Lake toddlers to manage their attention by attending alternately to several competing events, $t(20) = 2.5$, $p < .01$ (see Table 4 above and Fig. 21), although they did not differ in attending to several competing events simultaneously. Salt Lake toddlers were more likely to appear unaware of ongoing events (other than that on which they were focused) than were Dhol-Ki-Patti toddlers, $t(25) = 3.4$, $p < .01$.

The Dhol-Ki-Patti toddlers' patterns of attention management also differed from those of the San Pedro toddlers. Dhol-Ki-Patti toddlers tended to alternate their attention among events more often than the San Pedro toddlers, $t(16) = 3.1$, $p < .01$, while the San Pedro toddlers more often paid attention to several events simultaneously, $t(19) = 6.7$, $p < .0001$.

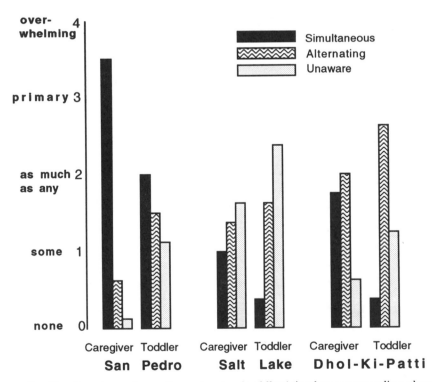

FIG. 21.—Rated prevalence of caregivers' and toddlers' simultaneous attending, alternating attending, or seeming unaware in San Pedro, Salt Lake, and Dhol-Ki-Patti.

Caregivers in Dhol-Ki-Patti were more likely than those in Salt Lake to attend to several events simultaneously, $t(25) = 2.4$, $p < .05$, as well as to alternate their attention between competing events, $t(24) = 2.1$, $p < .05$. The Salt Lake caregivers, in contrast, were more likely than the Dhol-Ki-Patti caregivers to appear unaware of competing events, $t(23) = 3.1$, $p < .01$.

Although comparisons between Dhol-Ki-Patti and Salt Lake supported our speculations that, in communities emphasizing observation, people are more likely to share their attention among competing events, comparisons between Dhol-Ki-Patti and San Pedro (both representing such communities) reveal that there are also differences in means of attention sharing. Whereas San Pedro caregivers tended to attend to several events simultaneously, Dhol-Ki-Patti caregivers were as likely to alternate their attention as to attend simultaneously (see Table 4 above). The differences between Dhol-Ki-Patti and San Pedro were significant, with San Pedro caregivers more often sharing their attention simultaneously between competing events, $t(18) = 6.9$, $p < .0001$, and Dhol-Ki-Patti caregivers more often alternating attention, $t(16) = 6.9$, $p < .0001$; the latter also more often appeared unaware of competing events, $t(15) = 2.5$, $p < .05$.

The vignette in which Ramu's father guided his actions with the jar and ring also illustrates how the father was able to attend to competing events simultaneously: he demonstrated the actions of opening and closing the lid and drew his son's attention to the ring inside the jar at the same time as he answered the research assistant's questions (see Fig. 14 above).

In another example, Lachmi's brother (who was about 4 years old) teased her by thrusting the puppet close to her face as if to startle or frighten her. Lachmi protested by whining and looking up at her mother with a complaining glance. Without looking at the brother, the mother held and pushed aside his hand to prevent him from thrusting the puppet at Lachmi while she simultaneously looked at Lachmi and said sympathetically, "He doesn't listen, does he?" (see Fig. 22).

Although the difference did not reach significance, Dhol-Ki-Patti toddlers (like San Pedro toddlers) did not interrupt their caregivers as frequently as did Salt Lake toddlers (in 5% of the episodes as compared to 19%, respectively). As caregivers often shared their attention among several ongoing events and were responsive and poised ready to help the toddlers, it may have been less necessary for toddlers to resort to interruption to get caregivers' attention.

Engaging embedded in a group versus being taught in a dyad.—The Dhol-Ki-Patti sample's tendency to attend to several competing events may relate to their being typically embedded in group relationships and almost always surrounded by other people and multiple ongoing events and activities. The Dhol-Ki-Patti toddlers' involvements more frequently reflected being

119

Fig. 22.—This Dhol-Ki-Patti mother illustrates simultaneous management of several activities, as she indicates to her son to remove his hand while she smiles at her little daughter, Chanda, and says sympathetically, "He doesn't listen, does he?"

embedded in group interactions (as opposed to dyadic interactions with individuals) than did those of the Salt Lake toddlers (in 41% of the Dhol-Ki-Patti episodes compared to 10% of the Salt Lake episodes, respectively, $t[16]$ = 2.8, $p < .01$; see Figs. 23 and 24). Dhol-Ki-Patti toddlers and caregivers often responded at once to several suggestions and instructions from the ubiquitous "audience," engaging simultaneously in several interactions.

In the following jar episode, a 2-year-old responded to suggestions from her mother and from an adult neighbor:

The mother opened the jar, and Lachmi smiled and took out the biscuit that was inside.

An adult neighbor told Lachmi to close the jar.

Lachmi picked up the lid and was about to place it on the jar when her mother asked her, "Are you going to eat it [the biscuit]?" Lachmi shook her head to her mother as she continued to place the lid on the jar in response to the neighbor's suggestion.

Now the neighbor suggested, "Then put the biscuit back in." At almost the same time the mother reassured Lachmi, "You can eat it."

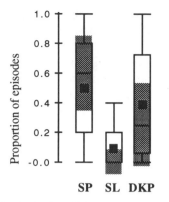

FIG. 23.—Proportion of episodes in which children evidenced engagement embedded in group activity in San Pedro (SP), Salt Lake (SL), and Dhol-Ki-Patti (DKP). For an explanation of the symbols, see the text.

Lachmi glanced at both adults and apparently decided to eat the biscuit.

Dhol-Ki-Patti toddlers were often alert and coordinating members of the group, monitoring and responding to concurrent actions and verbalizations from the group.

FIG. 24.—This Dhol-Ki-Patti toddler observes as both her mother and a teenage neighbor demonstrate the jumping jack and point out the relevant action to make it work.

OBSERVATIONS OF GUIDED PARTICIPATION: DRESSING AND
NOVEL OBJECT EXPLORATION DURING ADULT ACTIVITY

In this section, we discuss the extent to which the patterns of findings
from the novel object episodes are similar to those observed in the two other
situations of dressing and of novel object exploration during adult activity.
(The data on the variables coded in these situations appear in Tables 5–8
above.) As the data base is small, the analyses of these alternate situations
is very exploratory.

Dressing

Dressing was a familiar activity for Dhol-Ki-Patti caregiver-child interaction; caregivers were rarely uncomfortable or wary in this activity. Unlike
object-oriented play, dressing was not seen as being primarily within the
child's realm. Whereas caregivers treated the novel object activity as one
that was open ended and in which the child was free to explore or play
with the object in any way, they handled dressing as a structured task, with
clear steps to get the job done. They seemed to construe their role as being
responsible for getting the task done rather than as facilitating the child's
agenda or "teaching" the child self-help skills (see Fig. 25).

The pattern of between-community differences in the dressing episodes was for the most part consistent with that found in the novel object
episodes. However, there were a few notable departures from this pattern
that were related to the Dhol-Ki-Patti caregivers' differing approaches to
the two activities.

Whereas Dhol-Ki-Patti toddlers were more likely than Salt Lake toddlers to refuse or insist in the novel object episodes, the pattern was reversed
in the dressing episodes (see Table 7 above), where Dhol-Ki-Patti toddlers
refused or insisted less than did the Salt Lake toddlers (three episodes as
compared to eight episodes, respectively; in each case, the toddler was overruled by the caregiver). Further, whereas Dhol-Ki-Patti caregivers more
often remained poised ready to help than the Salt Lake caregivers during
the novel object episodes, there were no differences between the caregivers
from the two communities in the dressing episodes (see Table 7), consistent
with the notion that Dhol-Ki-Patti caregivers treated dressing as an activity
in which they were to control the agenda rather than facilitate the child's
agenda.

As with novel objects, Dhol-Ki-Patti caregivers tended to rely less on
verbal means of orienting to and simplifying the task of dressing than did
Salt Lake caregivers. However, the magnitude of between-community differences in caregivers' use of verbal means was smaller in the dressing epi-

Fig. 25.—This mother and older brother together dress a Dhol-Ki-Patti toddler after her bath.

sodes than in the novel object episodes. During dressing, Dhol-Ki-Patti caregivers used verbal means to orient toddlers in 64% of the episodes, as compared to 86% in the Salt Lake sample (see Table 5 above), whereas in the novel object episodes Dhol-Ki-Patti caregivers oriented verbally in 39% of the episodes, as compared to 74% in the Salt Lake sample. Dhol-Ki-Patti caregivers' use of more verbal means of orienting toddlers in the dressing situation may have been because they saw the dressing activity as requiring their direction.

Novel Object Exploration during Adult Activity

The pattern of data for novel object exploration during adult activity for Dhol-Ki-Patti and Salt Lake samples is consistent with the patterns of difference between San Pedro and Salt Lake (see Tables 5–8). The Salt Lake caregivers appeared to drop their organizational, instructional approach to the children when their primary focus was on their engagement with other adults. The Dhol-Ki-Patti caregivers maintained their supportive and attentive assistance in spite of being engaged in conversation with other adults, this perhaps being facilitated by the fact that much of the communication and support they provided for their toddlers involved subtle nonverbal means.

123

SUMMARY

Like caregivers and toddlers in San Pedro and Salt Lake, those in Dhol-Ki-Patti structured each other's involvement in interactions centered around all three types of activities—novel objects, dressing, and novel object exploration during adult activity. Caregivers oriented toddlers to the activity and simplified the task for them. Toddlers, in turn, structured the interactions by actively seeking greater involvement or assistance.

The pattern of differences in guided participation between the Dhol-Ki-Patti and the Salt Lake samples was generally consistent with expectations that we derived from the Dhol-Ki-Patti children's embeddedness in the adult world and the Salt Lake children's segregation from it. Dhol-Ki-Patti caregivers and toddlers were more likely than their Salt Lake counterparts to use subtle and complex nonverbal means of communication and less likely to use verbal means. Unlike Salt Lake caregivers, Dhol-Ki-Patti caregivers did not frequently provide language lessons to their toddlers. These patterns were generally the same in all three types of activities.

Dhol-Ki-Patti caregivers viewed their role during the novel object episodes as one of facilitating engagement with the objects—they demonstrated and instructed briefly and then turned the task over to the toddlers. They were not as likely as Salt Lake caregivers to engage in joint play as "playmates" of their children or to treat them as conversational peers. Dhol-Ki-Patti caregivers assumed the role of allowing the child to explore or work the novel objects independently while remaining poised ready to help when necessary. When toddlers refused or insisted (which they did more frequently than Salt Lake toddlers), caregivers did not appear to overrule them as often as did their counterparts in Salt Lake. Dhol-Ki-Patti caregivers seldom attempted to organize instruction using mock excitement to motivate children or to use praise to reward and maintain their involvement with the objects.

There were a few variations in the pattern of differences between Dhol-Ki-Patti and Salt Lake that may relate to Dhol-Ki-Patti caregivers' differing treatment of the novel objects and dressing activities. Dhol-Ki-Patti caregivers appeared to regard dressing as a task that they needed to ensure got done. Toddlers refused and insisted less than they did in the novel object episodes, and, in the few instances when they did, the caregivers overruled them. Further, caregivers did not remain poised ready to help as they did in the novel object episodes.

The results from all three types of activity support the proposition that, in cultural communities in which they learn through participation in ongoing adult activity, children are keen observers. Consistent with this, Dhol-Ki-Patti toddlers were more likely than Salt Lake toddlers to share their attention by focusing alternately on several competing events and less likely to appear unaware of other ongoing events. Similarly, Dhol-Ki-Patti caregivers were more likely than Salt Lake caregivers to attend to several events simultaneously. Dhol-Ki-Patti caregivers and toddlers were embedded in group interactions, aware of and responding to a group of people. The Dhol-Ki-Patti pattern of guided participation is similar to that observed in San Pedro and contrasts with that observed in Salt Lake.

VI. GUIDED PARTICIPATION IN KEÇIÖREN

Artin Göncü

The goal of this chapter is to investigate the similarities and differences in guided participation in Keçiören and in San Pedro and Salt Lake. The first section of the chapter describes Keçiören and provides information on the 14 families. The background information on Keçiören is based on Göncü's own experiences as someone who grew up there and on oral reports of the people who live in Keçiören. The information on the families comes from the interviews as well as from his shared history with some of these families. After summarizing cultural goals of development and patterns of age segregation, the chapter provides results of the observations of novel objects, dressing, and novel object exploration during adult activity episodes.

BACKGROUND OF THE COMMUNITY AND FAMILIES IN KEÇIÖREN

The site of observations in Turkey was Keçiören, one of the five major districts of the capital city, Ankara (which had a population of over 2 million in 1985, the time of data collection). Keçiören is 250 square km in size and has a population of about 600,000. When Ankara became the capital city in 1923, Keçiören was a sparsely populated countryside with vineyards and single-family dwellings, a summer resort for high-status bureaucrats and upper-class families. However, beginning in the early 1950s, Keçiören became a residential area for those who came to the city from nearby villages and small towns. The vineyards and single-family houses were gradually replaced by three- or four-story apartment buildings with two to four apartments on each floor. Typically, the apartments contain two or three bedrooms, a bathroom, a kitchen, and a family or living room with a dining table, coffee tables, television, radio, and chairs. Of the 14 families involved in the present study, 13 lived in such apartments, and one lived in a two-family dwelling. Half the families owned their own residences.

Some Keçiören families have lived in the city for two or three generations, while others still have ties with their rural relatives. Indeed, a couple of the mothers in our sample were born and lived in the villages before they came to the capital as brides. Parents in only three families had lived in another country or in another Turkish city before they moved to Ankara.

Currently, Keçiören is populated by mostly middle- to upper-class families, with men's occupations varying from college professor to factory worker and no family being either extremely wealthy or extremely poor. Most of the men commute to work in the city center of Ankara (about 8 km away), using public transportation; few have cars. The present sample was representative of this mixture of professions. Of the 14 fathers, three were professionals (a lawyer, a college professor, and an executive), three were small business owners (a furniture maker, a grocer, and a spice-shop owner), one was a professional soccer player, and the remaining eight were merchants, salesmen, or skilled workers.

Most women in Keçiören are homemakers. This was evident in the present sample, in which 13 were homemakers and one a bank teller. The mothers are almost always solely responsible for child care and household chores. A typical day in the lives of the women includes socializing with relatives, neighbors, and friends in settings such as shopping markets and homes. The women often gather for morning coffee or afternoon tea, rotating from house to house, exchanging news and recipes and providing social support.

Almost all the residents of the district are Muslim (varying from religious to liberal), along with a minority of Armenian Christians. Of our 14 families, 12 were Muslims, and two were Christian. All families in the district speak Turkish at home, with some older Christians using a disappearing dialect of Armenian.

Most of the families are nuclear; 11 were so in the present sample. Only three families were extended, with grandparents living with the families. However, nine of the 11 nuclear families had relatives living either in the same neighborhood or in the same city. All toddlers in the sample had both parents living in the same household. The average ages of the mothers and fathers were 26.5 and 31.5 years, respectively. Eight children had siblings, and one child had a younger sibling. Only one of the children was still nursing (eight had stopped before 3 months or never nursed; five had stopped after 3 months). No children had died in any of the families.

In Keçiören, children often do not attend preschool or kindergarten but rather stay home with their mothers, as was the case for all but one toddler in our sample. If the mother works outside the home, another family member takes care of the child—usually a grandmother or an aunt.

Children socialize together in the yards, streets, parks, and schoolyards. They start schooling at age 6 years in the public school system, with the goal of obtaining the elementary school diploma that is required by the Turkish government. Schooling beyond the fifth grade is optional in Turkey.

Age Segregation

Indices of age segregation reflect the Keçiören families' transitory state between their rural roots and urban living. The toddlers varied in their sleeping arrangements: one child slept in the same bed with the parents, nine slept in the same room as their parents but in their own beds, two slept with other family members such as grandmothers, and two had their own rooms. However, even children who had their own rooms fell asleep in the company of others before being carried to their own beds. Possibly because of not having to fall asleep alone, the majority (13) of the Keçiören toddlers did not have bedtime routines, and only one had an attachment object.

Children are totally segregated from the adults' economic work life; they are never in the parents' workplace either as participants or as observers. No income-producing activity takes place at home.

These facts suggest that, in Keçiören, children are in the process of becoming segregated from adults, which contrasts with rural life in Turkey, where children are not segregated from the adult world. In fieldwork preparatory for a project published by Balamir-Bazoglu (1982), Göncü was told that village toddlers of this age often sleep with parents or grandparents and are involved in the social and economic activity of the adults either as observers or as participants.

Goals of Development

The goals for children's development in Keçiören also reflect the transition from rural roots to urban living. One of the three most common goals, expressed in the form of a motto, reflects a traditional rural value common to many communities in Turkey: "Respect the older and love the younger." The Keçiören mothers were already teaching their children how to express respect by adopting proper manners, such as in greeting house guests. We saw several instances during our visits; for example, with the mothers' encouragement, children who could talk referred to me in appropriate terms as *agbi* (older brother) or *amca* (uncle). Some of the children greeted us in the traditional way by first holding and kissing our right hands and then touching the hand with their foreheads in a gesture of bowing. Some would pour lemon cologne into our hands after we had eaten, in a traditional ritual for treating guests. Almost all waved their hands in saying good-bye as we left their homes.

The second developmental goal of these families reflects their desire that their children become part of urban life by obtaining a college education and entering a prestigious profession. This was true for all parents (whose own educational level varied from fifth grade to college graduate). Twelve of the mothers specified the profession that they wished their children to enter: 11 wanted their child to become a medical doctor, and one wanted her son to be a businessman.

The emphasis on formal education as a goal for children's development is also evident in the historical change in educational level of the women in these families. The mothers in our sample had attended 9 years of school on the average (equal to their husbands). Every mother had more schooling than her own mother. Thus, if the grandmother had had no schooling, the mother had an elementary school diploma; if the grandmother had some schooling or an elementary school education, the mother had at least some middle or high school education.

This generational change in level of formal education is reflected not only in the mothers' wish that their children become professionals but also in patterns of mother-child interaction. One of the mothers expressed this most directly by saying, "In school we learned about child development and child language; we learned that playing with children is good for them." Consistent with this statement, mothers commonly reported acting as play partners to their toddlers, 11 indicating that either they or the fathers played with the children; only three reported that other children were their toddlers' sole playmates. In acting as play partners to their children, these mothers differed from their own mothers. Because of my personal relationships with some of the grandparents, I know that playing with children was not a common way of interacting with the toddlers who are now the mothers in our sample. For the grandmothers, playing with youngsters—especially in pretense—is something that children do among themselves. This is consistent with the views expressed in San Pedro as well as with my observations of Turkish peasants.

The Keçiören mothers' emphasis on play was also evident in their children's toys, which included stuffed animals, block puzzles, electric trains, backgammon sets, and dolls. (For an illustration of a game being played by a mother and a toddler, see Fig. 26.)

Raising skilled children was the third goal of development in Keçiören. This was expressed in the context of talking about teaching children how to take care of household chores and attempting to accelerate the pace of

FIG. 26.—Keçiören mothers entered into play with children as peers, such as in this game of backgammon.

their development. Half the mothers (largely those of the older toddlers) mentioned that they encouraged their children to be actively involved in household chores such as dusting furniture and sweeping floors. All noted making special efforts to facilitate their children's development; nine reported that they actively instructed their toddler in how to walk and talk, and five reported encouraging their children in these skills. The toddlers in the sample varied in their passing of milestones. Four children had completed toilet training, seven were in the process, and three had not begun. Five children were in the process of learning to walk, and nine were already skilled walkers. Four children were reported to say one or two words, five to say three to six words, two to say seven or more words, and three to be combining words.

OBSERVATIONS OF GUIDED PARTICIPATION: NOVEL OBJECTS

Preliminary Analyses

Keçiören toddlers made more interactional moves, averaging nearly 20 per episode, than either the San Pedro or the Salt Lake toddlers, who averaged between 10 and 20. This may have been due to Keçiören mothers' interest in fostering their children's development through play and in exhibiting their toddlers' competence.

The toddlers' interactive partners consisted almost exclusively of adults; child partners were present in an average of only 1% of the episodes. This differs sharply from the situation in San Pedro, $t(13) = 3.1, p < .01$. Although fathers and grandmothers were around to interact with the toddlers in a few cases, mothers were always children's principal partners, reflecting their interpretation of novel objects exploration as a task involving only the toddlers and themselves.

Cultural Similarities in Guided Participation

Creating Bridges

There is a striking similarity of results obtained in Keçiören on measures of creating bridges between caregivers and children's understanding of the activity with those of San Pedro and Salt Lake. Mutual involvement in Keçiören occurred in an average of 87% of the episodes, like the San Pedro average of 89% and the Salt Lake average of 81%. Orientation to the task occurred in almost all episodes in all three communities: 99% in Keçiören, 99% in San Pedro, and 96% in Salt Lake. These data support the idea that guided participation through bridging is common across different communities.

Structuring

The similarities in caregivers and children structuring each others' activities parallel those in bridging: Keçiören mothers, like San Pedro and Salt Lake caregivers, usually simplified the job of their children (in 91%, 93%, and 87% of the episodes, respectively). Their toddlers were also similar in the extent of structuring the activity. Keçiören toddlers, like those in San Pedro and Salt Lake, introduced information or structure (in an average of 41%, 33%, and 29% of the episodes, respectively), sought involvement (in an average of 94%, 89%, and 79% of the episodes), and sought assistance (in an average of 31%, 43%, and 33% of the episodes). Statistical tests conducted on seeking involvement and assistance (reliability for *introduces information or structure* was low) revealed no significant differences between communities.

The similarities in bridging and structuring across Keçiören, San Pedro, and Salt Lake provide further support for our central thesis that these processes of guided participation extend beyond cultural boundaries.

Cultural Variation in Guided Participation

Means of Communication and Instruction

Verbal and nonverbal communication.—The differences in patterns of communication in Keçiören and San Pedro mirror for the most part those in Salt Lake and San Pedro (for means and standard deviations, see Table 1 above). Keçiören mothers, like Salt Lake caregivers, spoke an average of four to nine sentences to their toddlers; in comparison to San Pedro caregivers, they talked significantly more, $t(16) = 3.6$, $p < .01$ (see Fig. 27). Compared with Keçiören, in San Pedro there were 11 times as many episodes with three or fewer sentences, whereas episodes with more than 10 sentences occurred nearly three times as often in Keçiören as in San Pedro.

The average amount of talk by the Keçiören toddlers was also higher than that of the San Pedro toddlers; like the Salt Lake toddlers, children in Keçiören produced one to three words per episode. The difference between San Pedro and Keçiören, tested in an age × community ANOVA (following the San Pedro–Salt Lake comparison as a model) was significant, $F(1, 25) = 4.4$, $p < .05$.

The emphasis of Keçiören mothers on guiding their children by spoken means is evident in their verbal orienting and simplifying (see Fig. 28). These mothers oriented their children by verbal means significantly more than the San Pedro caregivers, $t(22) = 1.8$, $p < .05$; the relative frequency of nonverbal means of orientation did not differ in the two samples. The

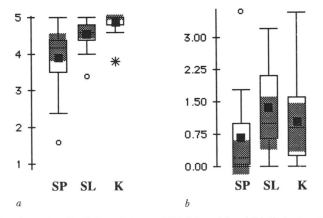

Fig. 27.—Amount of talk by adults to child (*a*) and by child (*b*) in San Pedro (SP), Salt Lake (SL), and Keçiören (K). For an explanation of the symbols, see the text. Rating scale of amount of talk to child: (3) = 1–3 sentences; 4 = 4–9 sentences; 5 = 10+ sentences. Rating scale of amount of talk by child: 0 = no words; 1 = 1—3 words; 2 = 4+ words; 3 = 1–3 phrases; 4 = 4+ phrases.

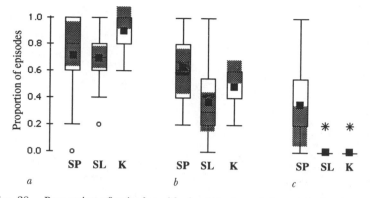

Fig. 28.—Proportion of episodes with simplification of the activity by the caregiver through means of verbal statements (*a*), gestures (*b*), or gaze, touch, posture, or timing cues (*c*) in San Pedro (SP), Salt Lake (SL), and Keçiören (K). For an explanation of the symbols, see the text.

Keçiören mothers used verbal simplification significantly more than both the San Pedro, $t(18) = 1.9$, $p < .05$, and the Salt Lake caregivers, $t(21) = 2.6$, $p < .05$. However, they simplified less with gesture, $t(23) = 1.9$, $p < .05$, and with gaze, touch, posture, or timing cues, $t(13) = 4.7$, $p < .001$, than the San Pedro caregivers.

The following interaction between 14-month-old Hüseyin and his mother illustrates the Keçiören emphasis on talk (Fig. 29 shows Hüseyin's mother explaining how the hoop works):

Hüseyin's mother separated the pieces of the hoop and told him playfully, "If you squeeze these, the inner piece comes apart." He grabbed the inner piece from her, and she extended the outer piece to him, saying, "Take this and put them together."

Hüseyin took them, and his mother invited him several times to "put them together."

When Hüseyin refused, whining, his exasperated mother questioned, "Why?" in amazement.

Then Hüseyin shifted the activity as he held the pieces as a steering wheel and made "nnnnnnn" Turkish driving sounds in response, pretending to drive, and his mother responded in a high pretend voice, "Oh, this is a car...."

Toddlers also demonstrated cultural differences in means of communication (see Fig. 30). Although Keçiören and San Pedro toddlers did not differ in seeking assistance by verbal means, which neither group used with any frequency, the Keçiören toddlers sought assistance through gesture,

Fig. 29.—Keçiören mothers heavily relied on explanations, such as, "If you squeeze these, the inner piece comes apart."

$t(21) = 3.1$, $p < .01$, as well as through gaze, touch, posture, or timing, $t(15) = 4.2$, p $< .001$, significantly less often than the San Pedro toddlers.[14]

In summary, the paramount means of communication in Keçiören is the word, with relatively little emphasis on gestural and other nonverbal means of communication. The emphasis placed by the women of Keçiören on talk in interacting with their children reflects their preparation of the children for schooling that stresses explicit verbal communication; it contrasts with the traditional value expressed in a proverb, "If word is silver, then silence is gold."

Explanation and demonstration.—Consistent with the view that Keçiören mothers' talk to their children had an educational purpose, these mothers more frequently provided explanations extending the current situation to another context than did San Pedro caregivers, $t(22) = 4.2$, $p < .001$ (for means and standard deviations, see Table 2 above; see also Fig. 31).

Extending to other situations with which the learner is familiar is very common among urban Turkish people, who often begin instruction with an analogy. The cultural difference may also relate to the Keçiören mothers' emphasis on schooling, which characteristically relies on explanation out of

[14] This difference should be interpreted cautiously since this variable could not be evaluated for reliability in the Keçiören data.

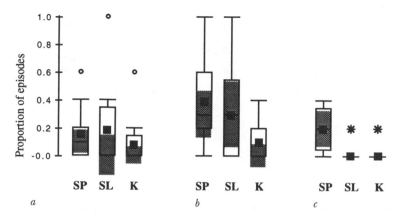

Fig. 30.—Proportion of episodes in which the toddler sought assistance by means of verbal requests (*a*), gestures (*b*), or gaze, touch, posture, or timing cues (*c*) in San Pedro (SP), Salt Lake (SL), and Keçiören (K). For an explanation of the symbols, see the text.

context. The following example illustrates the extent of Keçiören mothers' extending (see Fig. 32):

> One of the mothers told her 24-month-old daughter, Sevda, "Let's do beep beep," moving the hoop like a steering wheel. Then the mother extended to another situation by telling Sevda, "Remember, this is like your uncle's car, beep, nnnnn," as Sevda pretended to drive.
> Shortly after, Sevda put the hoop on her head, and her mother provided a comment extending this use of the hoop, "Simiiiiit," likening the child's gesture to that of a *simit* seller.[15]

There were differences between the two communities in caregivers' use of demonstration before the activity (see Fig. 31 above): Keçiören mothers provided significantly less advance demonstration than the San Pedro caregivers, $t(23) = 3.2$, $p < .01$. However, the two groups gave almost equal amounts of demonstration during the activity.

Both groups directed the children's attention to an ongoing process equally frequently; however, San Pedro caregivers turned over the activity to children significantly more often than the Keçiören mothers, $t(25) = 3.8$, $p < .001$. The Keçiören mothers may have been less likely to do so because of a desire to make sure that the children learned how to work the objects.

In sum, consistent with their emphasis on verbal rather than nonverbal communication, Keçiören mothers provided more explanation and less demonstration than the San Pedro caregivers.

---

[15] A *simit* is more or less a sesame-seed bagel, which is often carried on a tray placed on the seller's head.

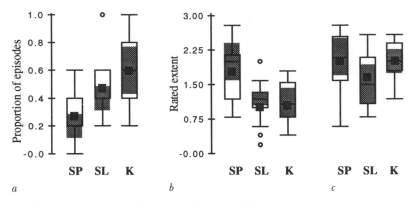

FIG. 31.—The extent to which caregivers extended the activity to other situations (*a*) and provided demonstration before (*b*) or during (*c*) children's participation in the activity in San Pedro (SP), Salt Lake (SL), and Keçiören (K). For an explanation of the symbols, see the text.

Adult-Child Roles in Teaching and Learning

Status equals in play.—Like Salt Lake caregivers, Keçiören mothers were often playmates to their toddlers—in 63% of the episodes, significantly more than the 7% observed for the San Pedro caregivers, $t(16) = 6.0$, $p <$ .0001 (for means and standard deviations, see Table 3 above; for a graphic presentation, see Fig. 33).

The following exchange provides an example of how Keçiören mothers played with their children:

> A mother introduced a game in which she and her 14-month-old daughter, Lamia, took turns putting the embroidery hoop on each other's head and then dropping it on the floor. The mother created a sense of pretend excitement by saying, "Ay, ay ay . . . ," each time they dropped the hoop. This was followed by joint laughter. The game became explicitly pretend when the mother put the hoop on Lamia's head, making the girl look like a bug with the handles of the hoop sticking out like antennas. The older brother chipped in, saying, "Lamia is a bug, Lamia became a bug." "What kind of a bug?" asked the mother in a coquettish way. "A lady bug," the mother and brother said simultaneously.

Our observations of Keçiören mothers acting as playmates with their children are consistent with their reports and with the observations of Salt Lake parents, suggesting that middle-class parents consider playing with their children to be part of their parental role.

Adults teaching versus supporting children learning.—Keçiören mothers re-

a

b

FIG. 32.—a, This Keçiören mother extended the exploration of the hoop to using it as a steering wheel, turning it like a steering wheel and commenting, "This is like your uncle's car." b, Soon, she extended the activity to another by likening the toddler's gesture to that of a *simit* seller.

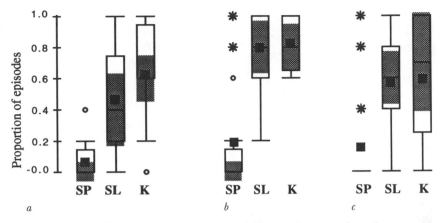

Fig. 33.—The proportion of episodes in which caregivers acted as playmates (a), adults conversed with child as peer (b), and child conversed with adults as peers (c) in San Pedro (SP), Salt Lake (SL), and Keçiören (K). For an explanation of the symbols, see the text.

sembled Salt Lake caregivers in acting as conversational partners with their children and in making efforts to motivate their children to engage in the activities.

Keçiören mothers acted as their toddlers' conversational partners in an average of 83% of the episodes, more frequently than the San Pedro caregivers, who were conversational partners in an average of 19% of the episodes, $t(19) = 6.2$, $p < .0001$ (see Fig. 33). Similarly, Keçiören toddlers more frequently adopted conversational peer roles with their mothers (in 60% of the episodes) than did San Pedro toddlers (in 16% of the episodes, $t[25] = 3.1$, $p < .01$).

The conversational peer roles taken by the Keçiören mothers and their children resembled dialogues in foreign language classes. For example, a mother holding the pencil box in front of her 23-month-old son asked sweetly and with mock excitement in her voice, "Aaaaa, Iskender, what's this?" The boy calmly replied, "It's a toy."

Teaching language occurred frequently in Keçiören. An average of 89% of the Keçiören episodes contained babytalk, significantly more than in San Pedro, where babytalk occurred in an average of 30% of the episodes, $t(20) = 4.7$, $p < .0001$ (see Fig. 34). The Keçiören mothers were extremely animated in talking to their children; they fluctuated the pitch of their voices, modulated their tone, simplified words, repeated sounds, and even sang in the course of keeping their children engaged in conversation. They were so dramatic that at times all of us, including the toddlers, burst into laughter.

The extent of vocabulary lessons in Keçiören was much greater than in San Pedro, $t(25) = 4.6$, $p < .0001$, similar to the contrast between Salt Lake and San Pedro (see Fig. 34). Keçiören mothers more frequently labeled objects (averaging 50% vs. 16% in San Pedro), requested labels (30% vs. 6%), provided running commentary (77% vs. 21%), expanded child speech (49% vs. 13%), and engaged in language games (16% vs. 4%). The toddlers mirrored the differences between the caregivers of the two communities, with the Keçiören toddlers participating in vocabulary lessons significantly more than the San Pedro toddlers, $t(21) = 2.3$, $p < .05$.

Two other types of language lessons were common in Keçiören. The first of these was requesting parroting—asking the child to repeat words—which the mothers did in 33% of the episodes. For example, one of the mothers prompted her 12-month-old boy, "Say good-bye to *agbi*. 'Good-bye *agbi*.' " The other type was singing, which occurred in about half the sample. Keçiören mothers sang lullabies, nursery rhymes, and adult songs to their children, emphasizing the words and encouraging the children to do so also. For example, one mother used a standard nursery rhyme to teach her 16-month-old daughter, Serap, new vocabulary when they were exploring the cone puppet. The mother sang several times, "Little frog, little frog, where are your ears? I don't have ears, I don't have ears, I live in creeks!" After each time, the mother asked Serap to repeat certain words, such as "little frog" (see Fig. 35).

Supporting the notion that they explicitly organized their children's learning, Keçiören mothers tried to motivate their children to explore the novel objects (see Fig. 36). Like the Salt Lake mothers, they more often attempted to motivate the children through mock excitement, $t(25) = 7.1$, $p < .0001$, and praise, $t(19) = 2.9$, $p < .01$, than the San Pedro mothers.

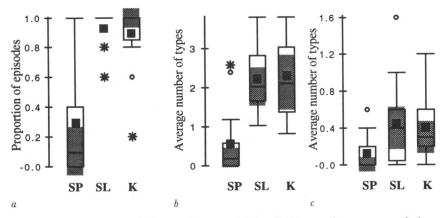

FIG. 34.—Extent to which caregivers used babytalk (*a*), caregivers gave vocabulary lessons (*b*), and child engaged in vocabulary lesson (*c*) in San Pedro (SP), Salt Lake (SL), and Keçiören (K). For an explanation of the symbols, see the text.

Fig. 35.—This Keçiören toddler repeats vocabulary words in a nursery rhyme on her mother's request to sing with her as they explore the frog emerging from the cone puppet.

In the following example, the mother of 23-month-old Kadir illustrates the use of praise in Keçiören (see Fig. 37):

> As Kadir pulled one of the legs of the jumping jack to make him move, his mother said several times, "Pull the string, don't hold his feet."
> Kadir followed the mother's instructions and managed to work the toy, and his mother complimented his accomplishment by saying, "That's right! You did it beautifully."
> Kadir followed this up with his own showing off by smiling and holding the toy in the air with pride toward the visitors.[16]

The stronger emphasis placed by Keçiören than San Pedro caregivers on organizing their children's learning surfaced in two other findings. First, Keçiören mothers were significantly less likely to be poised ready to help than were San Pedro caregivers, $t(25) = 2.5$, $p < .01$ (see Fig. 36 above). The Keçiören mothers were almost always already actively helping the children! The Keçiören mothers were poised ready to help more frequently

[16] Keçiören children praised themselves and showed off significantly more than San Pedro toddlers, $t(15) = 4.7$, $p < .001$. The children seemed to be expressing their understanding of mothers' praise through a similar action of self-praise, showing off their accomplishments. It seemed that children learned from their mothers to praise themselves as they learned to work the novel objects.

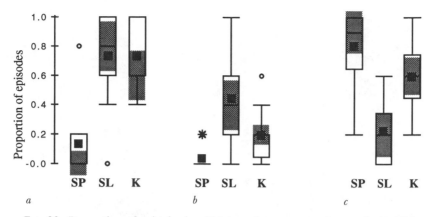

Fig. 36.—Proportion of episodes in which caregivers attempted to motivate children with mock excitement (*a*) or praise (*b*) and were poised ready to help children (*c*) in San Pedro (SP), Salt Lake (SL), and Keçiören (K). For an explanation of the symbols, see the text.

than the Salt Lake caregivers, $t(25) = 4.4$, $p < .001$. The Keçiören families' efforts to organize their children's learning is another indication of their transitional status to urban from village life, where such practices would be less common.

A second indication of the Keçiören mothers' efforts to manage their children's learning was the fact that they were significantly more likely to overrule the child than were the San Pedro caregivers, $t(23) = 4.4$, $p < .0001$ (see Table 3 above). The Keçiören mothers wanted to teach how to work the toys regardless of children's refusals. For example, the mother of 16-month-old Leyla tried to get her to play the jar as if it were a drum; when Leyla refused by whining, her mother overruled her refusal by holding the child's hands to get her to play the "drum."

In summary, the interactions of Keçiören toddlers and their mothers were for the most part similar to those we observed in Salt Lake City and dissimilar to those seen in San Pedro. Keçiören mothers interact with children on the children's own level, engaging in conversation, play, and baby-talk with them, and actively organize children's learning by explaining, motivating, and insisting, without necessarily turning the task over to the children.

Learning through Observation

Management of attention.—The attention patterns in Keçiören are intermediate between those characteristic of San Pedro and of Salt Lake (see

MONOGRAPHS

Fig. 37.—This Keçiören mother supported and praised her toddler's accomplishment in working the jumping jack, leading him to show off his success.

Fig. 38), possibly again reflecting these families' transitional state from a rural to an urban Turkish way of living. In most Turkish villages, children grow up in the company of others, with opportunities to learn from simultaneously occurring events, whereas, in urban Turkey, children receive instructions to focus on one event at a time.

In comparison to the toddlers of San Pedro, Keçiören toddlers were less likely to pay attention to competing events simultaneously, $t(13) = 8.5$, $p < .0001$, but more likely to alternate their attention, $t(21) = 4.1, p < .001$ (for means and standard deviations, see Table 4 above). There were no differences in the degree to which toddlers from Keçiören and San Pedro appeared unaware of competing events, whereas the Salt Lake toddlers were more likely to appear unaware of such events than those from San Pedro. In comparison to the toddlers of Salt Lake, Keçiören toddlers were significantly less likely to appear unaware of competing events, $t(25) = 2.0$, $p < .05$, and significantly more likely to alternate their attention, $t(25) = 2.9$, $p < .01$. A segment of Lamia's session exemplifies the alternating pattern of attention of the Keçiören toddlers:

> While Lamia and her mother concentrated on naming the pictures on the pencil box, Lamia alternated her attention between her focus on the pencil box and lifting her head to monitor the adults who were chatting in the background. Once while exploring the pencil box she

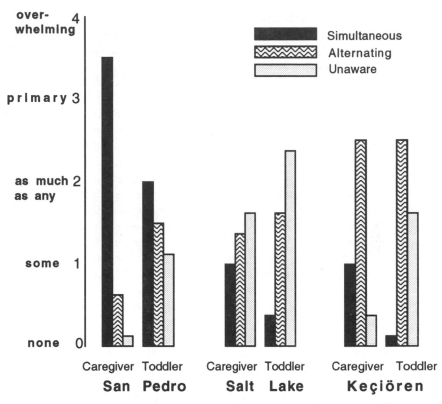

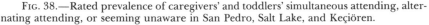

Fig. 38.—Rated prevalence of caregivers' and toddlers' simultaneous attending, alternating attending, or seeming unaware in San Pedro, Salt Lake, and Keçiören.

noticed me play with her stuffed animal and shouted as she pointed at the toy for me to give it to her, in another instance of alternating her attention between two foci.

The Keçiören caregivers followed the same intermediate pattern of attention management as their toddlers. Compared with the San Pedro caregivers, the mothers in Keçiören paid simultaneous attention significantly less frequently, $t(25) = 15.5$, $p < .0001$, and alternated significantly more, $t(18) = 11.9$, $p < .0001$. The two groups did not differ in appearing unaware of competing events, unlike the pattern for Salt Lake, where the caregivers appeared more frequently unaware than in San Pedro. Compared with the Salt Lake caregivers, the Keçiören mothers alternated significantly more, $t(22) = 4.4$, $p < .001$, and were unaware of competing events significantly less, $t(17) = 4.5$, $p < .001$.

These findings are consistent with the idea that the structures of the communities involve different patterns of learning and attention. In the life of Keçiören mother-toddler pairs, events tend to occur sequentially rather than simultaneously, perhaps owing to the nuclear, small, and private family structure as well as age and work segregation. This might account for the fact that caregivers and children in Keçiören were less likely to attend to competing events simultaneously and more likely to do so alternately than those in San Pedro. The Keçiören families' greater frequency, compared with those from Salt Lake, of attending to competing events alternately and lesser frequency of appearing unaware of them may reflect their recent shift from rural Turkish patterns of learning to urban middle-class living. Perhaps the rural attentional pattern of monitoring events would involve more simultaneous attention, and the extent of alternating attention between events may reflect a transition to the more exclusive focus of attention characteristic of the Salt Lake middle-class families, who often did not share attention among competing events. Or alternating attention may be simply another form of attention management, not an intermediate form of attention between simultaneous attention and appearing unaware of competing events.

Engaging embedded in a group versus being taught in a dyad.—As expected, the Keçiören children did not interact in a way that indicated that they were embedded in group activity as often as the San Pedro children, $t(19) = 3.6$, $p < .001$ (see Fig. 39). Since Keçiören children live in independent family units and have limited access to groups, it is not surprising that they less frequently engage as active participants when they are in the presence of a group. Also, it is plausible that these families emphasize dyadic interaction more than group interaction as a result of their emphasis on schooling,

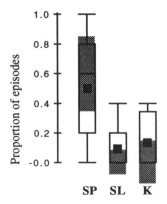

FIG. 39.—Proportion of episodes in which children evidenced engagement embedded in group activity in San Pedro (SP), Salt Lake (SL), and Keçiören (K). For an explanation of the symbols, see the text.

which encourages dyadic adult-child interaction either between single students and a teacher or between the class as a unit and the teacher.

OBSERVATIONS OF GUIDED PARTICIPATION: DRESSING AND NOVEL OBJECT EXPLORATION DURING ADULT ACTIVITY

Dressing

The Keçiören mothers and children treated the dressing activity differently than they did the exploration of novel objects. Nonetheless, the overall differences in patterns of interaction between Keçiören and San Pedro were similar for dressing to those observed for novel objects.

For the Keçiören mothers, dressing was a task that needed getting done, contrasting with the exploration of novel objects, which was a playful learning activity. They engaged in conversation, play, vocabulary lessons, babytalk, and praise less frequently during dressing than during novel object episodes. The fact that all nine mothers whose children refused to get dressed overruled that refusal attests to the idea that the mothers saw the dressing situation as a job that needed to get done. The following example of 25-month-old Silva illustrates how Keçiören mothers seemed to see dressing as a task to be performed without much play, conversation, or praise (however, as noted below, Keçiören mothers still did all these things more in dressing than did San Pedro caregivers):

> As her mother took off her shirt by pulling it over her head, Silva cooperated by lifting her arms. Silva's mother tapped on her shoulder for her to turn around so that the mother could put a dress on, and Silva did so and lifted one of her arms up as her mother began to put the dress over her head and one arm.
>
> The mother made her first verbal statement in the dressing episode by telling me that she had made the dress, when I asked.
>
> When she held the second sleeve of the dress for Silva to put her arm through, the child was not paying attention, and the mother, without saying anything, shook the sleeve to get her attention. Silva understood the mother's message and put her arm through the sleeve.

Because the Keçiören mothers' perception of dressing as a task led to a form of guidance that differed from what they offered in the exploration of novel objects, some differences between Keçiören and San Pedro families that characterized novel object episodes disappeared in the dressing episodes. The Keçiören mothers dropped in relative likelihood of orienting verbally and nonverbally in dressing compared with novel object episodes. They ceased extending, their talk to children became no more frequent than in San Pedro, and they ceased being poised ready to help. The San Pedro caregivers oriented and demonstrated more in dressing than the Keçiören mothers.

However, most of the differences that occurred between the two communities in the dressing episodes are consistent with those that we reported for the novel object episodes. Keçiören mothers continued to act as playmates and conversational peers, to use babytalk and praise, to give vocabulary lessons, and to overrule children more than the San Pedro caregivers. Keçiören children maintained their status as conversational partners. Keçiören mothers less frequently used gestural and gaze, touch, posture, and timing cues in simplification and demonstrated less frequently. Keçiören toddlers less frequently interacted in ways indicating that they were embedded in group activity.

Novel Object Exploration during Adult Activity

Since we did not tape all the interviews in Keçiören (owing to a shortage of videotape), the data are not comparable with those of San Pedro and Salt Lake, as there were few opportunities to observe novel object explorations during adult activity other than some embedded between novel objects episodes. Such instances arose in the sessions of only six families. Hence, interpretation of these data should be taken as merely suggestive.

In general, Keçiören mothers tended not to interact with their toddlers while they were interacting with adults. It is improper etiquette for a mother and child to interact with one another while the mother is talking to an adult. Thus, the mothers often used toys or sought help from other people to keep their children busy as they answered our interview questions. This tendency of Keçiören mothers to distinguish adult activity from child activity is consistent with how they focused their attention on one event at a time. When caregiver-child interaction did occur during adult conversation, it was often brief, as in the following example:

> As the mother was complaining to me about the noisy teenage girls living upstairs (who wear high heels at home!), her 14-month-old daughter, Azat, interrupted by vocalizing. The mother responded by giving Azat a piece of the nesting dolls and saying, "Close it in there." Azat played with the toy as we went back to conversation.

The Keçiören mothers' lesser focus on their children during adult activity than during the child-focused novel object episodes made the interactions in Keçiören and San Pedro more similar in that the Keçiören mothers' efforts to teach dropped off (except for their demonstration). However, certain differences still remained. Keçiören mothers were less frequently poised ready to help and to offer nonverbal assistance to their children than the San Pedro caregivers. Consistent with their caregivers' less available assistance, the Keçiören toddlers sought assistance less frequently than they had in the novel object episodes, whereas such requests remained high in San Pedro (where caregivers routinely attended simultaneously to interaction with their children and with adults). The Keçiören mothers continued to overrule their children.

In summary, these findings suggest that the San Pedro caregivers and children were attentive to one another during adult talk, whereas the Keçiören mothers, like the Salt Lake caregivers, seemed to focus on the adult activity to the exclusion of interaction with the children.

SUMMARY

The findings from Keçiören are generally similar to those from Salt Lake, but they also reflect these families' transitional state from a rural to an urban way of living. The Keçiören families' emphasis on formal schooling, teaching, language development, verbal communication, explanation, and alternation in attention appears to be based on their emerging urban middle-class lives. The peer status roles adopted by mothers as playmates and conversational partners with their children and their organization of the children's learning through mock excitement and praise provide the strongest support for this interpretation. The Keçiören mothers' tendency to overrule their children's insistence and not to turn activity over to the children might also index these mothers' efforts to teach their children what they think is important in the context of middle-class urban life. Nevertheless, the Keçiören families retained some traditional values and interactional patterns that are common to rural communities in Turkey and that were observed in San Pedro and Dhol-Ki-Patti. This appeared most strongly in these families' age segregation in sleeping arrangements, attention management, and readiness to help, all of which were intermediate between the patterns seen in San Pedro and in Salt Lake.

In conclusion, our observations in Keçiören illustrate that guided participation is an evolving dynamic process to which mothers and their children both contribute in ways that simultaneously involve similarities as well as differences with other communities.

VII. SYNTHESIS AND DIRECTIONS

The work reported in this *Monograph* contributes empirical support for the speculation that, across communities, guided participation simultaneously involves both similarities (in bridging and structuring) and variations (in goals of development, means of communication, and asymmetries in adults' and children's responsibility for learning). The goals and means of guided participation in two middle-class communities involved an emphasis on verbal rather than nonverbal instruction and adult structuring of children's motivation and involvement in learning through adult play and conversation as peers with young children and through the provision of lessons. The means of guided participation in two non-middle-class communities involved greater explicitness of nonverbal communication, responsibility of children to learn with sensitive assistance from caregivers, skilled sharing of attention between competing events evidencing keen observation, and engagement as members embedded in group activity.

A secondary contribution of this *Monograph* is methodological. We have developed and examined our ideas through the systematic abstraction of patterns—a method of data analysis based on close ethnographic narrative analysis of individual cases combined with efforts to abstract patterns that can describe the data across individual cases—systematically combining the tools of qualitative and quantitative analysis. This is a method that can be applied to studies other than cultural comparisons; Rogoff and her colleagues have used it in research on middle-class children's planning in laboratory and naturalistic situations and in staged and unstaged interactions in families and schools in various U.S. groups. The first study in a series necessarily relies more heavily on the ethnographic analysis of narrative descriptions of the activity, in order to develop an understanding of the basic shape of the patterns, and on thoughtfully developing the language of abstraction; subsequent related studies can build on these, adjusting the language of abstraction on the basis of briefer ethnographic analyses to fit the activity studied and extend the previous findings.

This final chapter begins by summarizing our findings regarding universals and variations in guided participation, emphasizing especially the two patterns of responsibility (children learning with assistance as opposed to adults teaching children) and differences in attention management. We then extend beyond the results to suggest that the two patterns we have found are likely to be oversimplified. We use ethnographic reports of children's learning through observation in a variety of communities to suggest directions that future work may take in further articulating how people become skilled observers. Finally, we consider the consequences of becoming skilled in learning through observation and participation in community activities as opposed to being engaged in lessons organized by adults, and we argue that people from differing communities could benefit from integrating the advantages available in both these approaches.

UNIVERSALS AND VARIATIONS IN GUIDED PARTICIPATION

In this study, we have focused on a situation in which toddlers and their caregivers participate together in several activities; we interpret our observations of their communication during the course of these activities in the context of the arrangement of children's activities in each community. Guided participation involves both such direct communication and the arrangements of activities in which children participate.

As suggested by Rogoff (in press), guided participation can be conceived as one plane of analysis in the understanding of how people function and develop in sociocultural contexts, one accompanying two other planes of analysis—processes of community change and individual change—that are inseparable from the plane of observation of interpersonal processes (here termed "guided participation"). Although focusing on just one plane is possible, the other two planes of analysis must appear as background for the whole to make sense. In other words, the processes of guided participation on which this *Monograph* has focused cannot be understood outside the context of both community/institutional processes and individual processes of development through participation; the three planes of analysis focus on mutually constituting processes, none of which are primary, but any of which can be foregrounded to form the focus of a particular study, with the others in the background. Although our focus has been on the interpersonal plane of analysis (interaction and interpersonal arrangements between children and their caregivers), we could not have conducted our analysis without background understanding of the community processes (e.g., the historical role and changing practices in each community of schooling, age segregation, families, and work) as well as the individual processes (e.g., learning through observation and participation in ongoing instructional and adult activities) to which we have also referred throughout this *Monograph*.

The results of our analyses support the idea that there are simultaneously important commonalities and differences in the processes of guided participation in varying cultural communities. The differences seem to relate both to community differences in schooling and age segregation and to differing patterns of learning through observation as opposed to through instruction. Research focusing more directly on the planes of analysis of cultural and individual processes will help fill out the picture.[17]

Universals

The aspects of guided participation that we found to occur across all four communities had to do with the collaboration between toddlers and their caregivers in bridging between their individual understandings of the situations at hand and in their structuring of each other's participation as they directly shared in problem solving as well as in their indirect decisions about the nature of their own and each other's participation in activities. Their guided participation included tacit and explicit forms of communication as well as distal arrangements of children's activities.

We argue that these commonalities across varying cultural communities are inherent to the nature of shared activity. In order to communicate and proceed toward common ends, it is necessary to develop some degree of shared understanding (through bridging) and to adjust one's own and one's partners' involvement (structuring). One of our aims is to focus attention on the everyday participation of all children in cultural practices in order to expand research beyond the explicit, didactic, self-conscious instructional interaction that has been the typical subject of investigation. The interdependence of children and their social partners in valued and routine cultural activities may account for children's rapid development as participants in the practices and understandings of their community, whether this involves learning to weave or to read, to tend to livestock or young children, or to do schoolwork.

Variations

Along with the universal processes that we argue characterize guided participation, there are also very important cultural variations, especially in the goals of development and the nature of involvement between children and adults. Variations across communities have to do with differing values

[17] A related study (Morelli, Rogoff, & Angelillo, 1992) supports the picture with observations of community differences in children's opportunities to observe and participate in adult activities vs. instruction in San Pedro, Salt Lake, Boston, and Zaire.

regarding such practices as literacy, academic discourse, and interpersonal coordination. Goals of development vary according to local practices and values along with having panhuman similarities.

In addition to documenting differences in the goals of development, our results support the notion that there are at least two patterns for learning the mature roles of a community that appear to be accompanied by variations in whether children are allowed to observe and participate in ongoing adult activities. In communities where they are segregated from adult activities, children's learning may be organized by adults' teaching of lessons and provision of motivational management out of the context of adult practice; in communities in which children are integrated in adult settings, learning can occur through active observation and participation by the children with responsive assistance from caregivers. We do not intend to draw causal connections between age segregation and adult versus child responsibility for learning; our aim is to examine patterns of connection between these two aspects of community differences in children's activities, which of course covary with many other community practices.

In the two communities in which children have the opportunity to observe and participate in adult social and work activities, caregivers appeared to support their toddlers' own efforts with responsive assistance, and toddlers appeared to take responsibility for observing ongoing events and beginning to enter adult activity. In the two communities in which children are usually segregated from adult activities, caregivers seemed to take responsibility for organizing children's involvement by managing their motivation and by instructing through the provision of lessons (especially in language use) and through play and conversation as peers with the toddlers.

The differences between communities were largely consistent across the three types of activity that we observed: operating novel objects when the caregiver was requested to help the child, operating a routine object (putting on a shirt) when requested to do so, and operating novel objects when the child was not the focus of adult attention and had not been requested to engage in the activity by the researcher. The primary difference between these activities was that the management of teaching by middle-class caregivers dropped off in the episodes of dressing and novel object exploration during adult activity, in which they may not have regarded their role as being instructional. By contrast, caregivers in the non-middle-class communities maintained their attentive and sensitive assistance to the children in all three types of activity, and the toddlers sustained alert involvement.

Thus, the instructional responsibility taken by middle-class caregivers appeared to be situationally bound: they organized instruction in a situation that called for helping a child learn, but in other situations, not only did they not organize instruction, but they also did not provide the sort of attentive and sensitive help that the caregivers from the other two communities provided in all three types of activity.

The interactions in the middle-class families, we argue, are similar to the type of interaction for which the children are being prepared to participate in school, where middle-class children will spend years of their lives out of the context of adult activity preparing for adulthood and for their economic and social position as adults. The middle-class children and their caregivers engaged in dyadic interactions that resemble school instruction, organized by the caregivers to motivate and teach the children. This is consistent with Haight's (1991) report that almost all the middle-class parents that she interviewed regarded pretend play and book reading as important activities for their 2-year-olds' cognitive and language development; many identified their own roles as teaching and encouraging development and preparing their toddlers for school (see also Farran, 1982).

In contrast, in the two communities in which children are able to observe and participate in adult activities, children took the responsibility for managing their efforts, with their caregivers acting as sensitive assistants. Our observations are consistent with earlier spot observations of 9-year-olds in San Pedro, in which native observers identified only six out of 1,708 occasions on which the children were explicitly being taught outside school and many occasions on which the children were competently engaged in household work (Rogoff, 1981a). In San Pedro and Dhol-Ki-Patti, children are not often segregated from adult economic and social activities; they observe from infancy and begin to contribute to ongoing adult economic and social activity even as toddlers. Under such circumstances, it may not be necessary for adults to organize specialized learning situations (in school and at home) to manage children's progress toward full participation in the activities of the community. Adults may not need to take the role of peers in play and conversation with tiny children in order to "bring" them up if children become keen observers of and skilled participants in the mature activities that surround them.

Nonetheless, in San Pedro, there may be changes in discourse practices occurring that relate to the community's increasing orientation to schooling: mothers with more than a sixth-grade education were more similar to those in Salt Lake in terms of the amount of talk with their toddlers, the amount of explanation given, and interacting with children as peers in play and in conversation.

There was, however, no relation between schooling and the extent to which the San Pedro caregivers shared their attention among competing events, a practice that we speculate supports learning through observation and participation. This suggests that attention patterns may be resilient cultural practices that are less open to quick change as a result of a few years of schooling; changes in attention management practices may take generations rather than years. Regardless of their amount of schooling, San Pedro mothers systematically observed and participated in all the events going on around them at the same time. This contrasted with the Salt Lake caregivers' (and children's) reliance on attending to one event at a time, with frequent apparent lack of awareness of other ongoing events. In fact, the *toddlers* in San Pedro shared their attention among competing events more often than did the *caregivers* in Salt Lake, a community with lesser emphasis on observation and greater emphasis on receiving instruction.

BEYOND TWO PATTERNS OF LEARNING THROUGH OBSERVATION OR INSTRUCTION

In this *Monograph*, we aimed to establish the coherence of two patterns: adults organizing children's learning and children managing their own learning through keen observation and participation. This we regard as just an initial step in articulating important cultural variations in this direction since it is likely that learning through observation is more complex than our study has indicated. Our analyses draw attention to the process of learning through observation, and we regard our study as unique in establishing the variation in means of attention management across different communities. Although brief references to attention differences in varying communities can be found in ethnographic reports (to which we refer below), to our knowledge this study is the first to undertake a close examination of participants' foci of attention.

Several aspects of our study suggest the possibility that there may be more than two patterns of attention management. Although our results fit our speculations that attention is more likely to be shared among competing events in communities in which children are expected to learn through observation, there were nonetheless differences among those communities in how attention was shared. San Pedro stands out from the other three communities in the extent to which caregivers and toddlers simultaneously attended to competing events. While this means of attention management occurred occasionally in Dhol-Ki-Patti and in Keçiören, the pattern there was for greater alternation of attention. Salt Lake caregivers and toddlers stood out for the frequency with which they appeared unaware of competing events.

These three types of attention management are apparently not points along a continuum, and the differences among communities are not completely aligned with our observations of age segregation and of adult versus child responsibility for learning. Thus, the pattern for attention management is not quite the same as that of other variables showing differences between middle-class and non-middle-class communities in that Dhol-Ki-Patti and Keçiören differed from both San Pedro and Salt Lake. Although these strong community differences appear to be related to an emphasis on learning through observation, the fact that Dhol-Ki-Patti differed from San Pedro and Keçiören from Salt Lake requires further consideration. An explanation may be that attention patterns are slower to change as a result of increased participation in schooling than are such school-related discourse patterns as conversing with toddlers as peers and organizing instruction for them. The pattern that we observed in Keçiören—where the mothers had had a good deal of schooling but their own mothers had not—may fit with our San Pedro observations that mothers' schooling related to a greater likelihood of extensive talk and of conversational peer and playmate relations between caregivers and toddlers but did not involve differences in attention management. Perhaps the Keçiören mothers have rapidly adopted the discourse patterns of schooling but are making a slower transition from rural Turkish attention patterns. Such an explanation would not apply to the Dhol-Ki-Patti pattern, however.

These considerations point to the likelihood that there may be several patterns of learning through observation and participation in ongoing community practices, not just the one that we have thus far contrasted with the middle-class approach.[18] We hope that our study will serve as an impetus to give greater attention to how people learn through observation and participation and that future work will help articulate a variety of cultural practices of support for learning through observation.

---

[18] Another finding that does not follow the main patterns concerns the caregivers' overruling as opposed to acceding to children's strongly expressed desires, which may have to do with cultural differences in who is ultimately responsible for children's actions and in concepts of respect for individual autonomy. In San Pedro, caregivers seldom overruled when children refused or insisted, a practice consistent with children's leadership role in learning and with a cultural respect for the autonomy of the individual. In the other three communities, caregivers overruled children in at least some situations. In Salt Lake and Keçiören, they did so in at least half of all types of episodes. Although the figures for Dhol-Ki-Patti were not sufficiently reliable to permit statistical analysis, it appeared that caregivers there did not overrule children's refusal or insistence in the novel object activity, which they seemed to regard as the children's domain, but usually did so in dressing, a situation that the caregivers seemed to regard as a task that needed to be done in a particular way. In Salt Lake, Dhol-Ki-Patti, and Keçiören, overruling the child's will may not be seen as a lack of respect for the child's autonomy in the way that it would be in San Pedro, where practices accord the ultimate responsibility for decisions to the individual. This topic has some importance in that it demonstrates that, in San Pedro, interdependence does not mean lack of autonomy, a concept that may differ from U.S. academic conceptions of independence but that fits with ethnographic observations in a variety of other communities, especially Native American (see Ellis & Gauvain, 1992; Lamphere, 1977; Mosier, Rogoff, & Chavajay, 1992).

How Do People Learn through Observation?

Investigation of specific attention patterns will require close *observation* of observation, a process that we have initiated in the present *Monograph*. We have employed careful (micro)ethnographic study of the observation processes appearing in the videotapes of families from varying communities, attempting to abstract patterns of community similarities and differences that are true to the situations and practices of the individuals and communities that were studied.

To extend our findings regarding differing cultural patterns of children's responsibility for learning and skill in observation, it is useful to examine ethnographic accounts that have focused on non-Western arrangements of children's development. Many of these observations support the idea of there being a connection between the opportunity to observe and participate in adult activities, the roles that adults take in supporting children's learning, and the children's own responsibility to pay keen attention to ongoing events and to become skilled participants in complex activities.

In many cases, children are taught to be keen observers by parents and other instructors, as occurs in learning through watching in Suzuki and school instruction in Japan (Peak, 1986) as well as during informal opportunities to learn through observation in a variety of communities. In some communities children are simply encouraged to observe, and in others (e.g., San Pedro) the aspects of an event that require closer attention are pointed out. Schieffelin (1991) noted that Kaluli (New Guinea) toddlers "are encouraged to notice and pay attention to situations with uncertain outcomes. . . . Adults tell children between 2 and 3 to indicate to the baby . . . that something is happening" (p. 92). Mothers in that community do not provide verbal instruction in how to carry out a task; young daughters spend a great deal of time observing their mothers and are asked to do specific jobs to facilitate a task, such as to bring fire tongs or turn bananas over on the fire. Mothers encourage this assistance and gradually add new jobs as the child gets older; daughters fill responsible roles at an early age, usually by 3 years. Mothers present a model of how a task is to be done and tell children to repeat the action, saying, "Do like that," demarcating separable actions or components of a task to punctuate separable points.

Coy (1989) reported a similar emphasis on focused observation in his description of his apprenticeship to a Kenyan blacksmith: "Occasionally, Magalgal [the master blacksmith] would call my attention to what he was doing to make certain that I was paying attention to something that he felt was important. He would say, 'now this is the difficult part,' and, that was my cue to attend to what he was doing" (p. 120).

In other communities that emphasize children's observation and participation, guided participation may involve adjustments made to facilitate children's efforts with little or no verbal explanation. Howard (1970) reported that Rotuman (Polynesian) children are subtly encouraged to imitate and that, if a child experiences difficulty, an adult may physically adjust the child's position to correct an error or refine a movement, seldom offering verbal instruction. If children ask for verbal instruction, "they are likely to be told to watch a skillful adult in action" (p. 116). Questions directed by children to adults (or apprentices to masters) are rare in some communities (Briggs, 1991; Goody, 1978; Heath, 1983). Goody speculated that U.S. middle-class children are taught to ask questions through the "training questions" (part of our *vocabulary lesson* variable) asked of them by their caregivers from infancy.

Rather than relying on questions and explanations to organize their learning, observers may be skilled in picking up information through watching, sometimes even without actually participating in carrying out the task. Nash (1967) reported that adults learn to use the footloom in a weaving factory in Guatemala by sitting beside a skilled weaver for a period of weeks, simply observing, asking no questions, and receiving no explanations. The learner may fetch a spool of thread from time to time for the weaver but does not begin to weave until, after weeks of observation, the learner feels competent to begin. At that point, the apprentice has become a skilled weaver simply by watching and by attending to whatever demonstrations the experienced weaver has provided.

Similarly, Collier (1988) reported that "Navajos do not teach their children, but they incorporate them in every life task, so that children learn themselves, by keen observation. Mothers do not teach their daughters to weave, but one day a girl may say, 'I am ready. Let me weave' " (p. 262). Black Elk described his own learning as a Sioux child: "The boys of my people began very young to learn the ways of men, and no one taught us; we just learned by doing what we saw, and we were warriors at a time when boys now are like girls. It was the summer when I was nine years old" (Niehardt, 1932, p. 17). Likewise, in a narrative based on his own Gikuyu upbringing prior to the introduction of European rule, Kenyatta (1953) described the importance in Gikuyu society of learning to be a keen observer and noted that Gikuyu parents took care to teach children to be good observers.

Observation as an Active Process of Peripheral Participation

In communities in which observation is possible and children are encouraged to be keen observers, people may be especially active and skilled in observation. Mainstream middle-class researchers, who may rely less on observation, tend to think of observation as being a passive process. However, our research suggests that skilled observation requires active management of attention. Observation is an aspect of the process that Lave and Wenger (1991) called "learning through legitimate peripheral participation." Fortes (1938/1970) reported that the Tallensi (of Ghana) explain rapid learning in terms of keen observation: "He has eyes remarkably." Briggs (1991) pointed out that Inuit children are expected to take the initiative in learning by observing closely, reasoning, and finding solutions independently, with self-motivation being the impetus.

Children in cultural communities that stress children's responsibility for learning may have the opportunity to observe and participate in the skills of the community (including language skills) and may develop impressive skills in observation, with less explicit child-centered interaction needed to integrate children in the activities of society. Henry (1955) suggested that there are societal differences in sensitivity to signals from many ongoing sources that call for awareness on several levels simultaneously; he tied his speculation to ethnographic observations of communities in which children are involved in a complex social community with multiple relationships.

Keen observation may promote understanding, facilitating, and managing complex social events. Briggs (1991) pointed out that good observers are skilled in anticipating the plans and direction of the group. Similarly, Ochs (1988) attributed the attentional skills of Samoan transcribers of audiotapes, who were able to follow three or four people talking simultaneously in different areas of a living space, to early socialization patterns in which children are expected to watch and listen to what is happening around them. She reported that, early in life, children are able to monitor others' conversations while carrying on their own.

Comparisons of Navajo and Euro-American 9-year-old children who were asked to teach 7-year-olds to play a game support the idea that skill in observation as well as in working in a group varies across communities (Ellis & Gauvain, 1992). Pairs of 9-year-old Navajo "teachers" were more likely to build on each other's comments than were Euro-American pairs, who more often offered two parallel, unrelated lines of instruction. The Navajo children provided a higher proportion of useful task information to total amount of information conveyed. They also gave evidence of more active observation, in that they remained engaged in the task, observing their partners even when they were not controlling the game moves; Euro-American children were distracted under such circumstances, sometimes to the point of leaving the task.

Several other accounts suggest that keen observation may promote skilled participation by young children. Sorenson (1979) noted that Fore (New Guinea) infants, whose caregivers are always accessible to them, have the responsibility of regulating contact by returning to "base" when they so desire. They have access to all aspects of the environment for observation and involvement and develop a realistic self-reliance. Adults intervene infre-

157

quently in their activities, to the point that children handle knives and fire safely by the time they are able to walk. Sorenson stated that he "continued to be surprised that the unsupervised Fore toddlers did not recklessly thrust themselves into unappreciated dangers, the way our own children tend to do" (p. 301). Similarly, Schieffelin (1991) observed that Kaluli 3–5-year-old girls would get together and collect firewood, make a small cooking fire, and cook themselves a bit of food and that Kaluli boys of this age had their own small pocket knives.

These reports suggest that, although people everywhere make a great deal of use of observation, there may be some communities in which observation skills are honed, where people make keen use of attention in learning how to participate in the practices of their community and to manage their interdependent involvement in rich social relations. Although we have contrasted school-like instruction with learning through keen observation and taking responsibility for one's own learning with the support of others, the two patterns of teaching and learning are not incompatible, as we discuss in the next section.

LEARNING FROM EACH OTHER: INTEGRATING DIFFERENT PATTERNS

Participation in the two patterns described in this *Monograph* may lead to varying success in managing one's own attention and observation, on the one hand, and in managing verbal interactions with adults as conversational peers, on the other. The utility of facility with these practices varies in different institutional contexts such as coordination with a group, formal schooling, and participation in ongoing economic activities.

Rather than regarding the two patterns that we have presented here as mutually exclusive, we argue that each can enrich the other. A sociocultural approach emphasizes that development occurs not just at the level of the individual but also at the level of societal change and that individuals and societies develop in part by borrowing practices from others. We conclude our discussion by speculating that participants in different communities may be able to expand their possibilities by cross-fertilization, by learning about and mastering forms of communication and learning that are not indigenous to their own community. We see this as multidirectional enhancement, with some communities learning from others how to engage in the discourse of schooling and the others learning from them how to engage in skilled observation of ongoing activities.

This notion has implications for participation in the institution of schooling. As traditional communities and minority communities in Western nations seek access to the economic institutions of middle-class Western nations, their children's involvement in schooling appears to be an inevitable step. Many observers have referred to the difficulties faced by non-middle-class children in Western schools as a problem of mismatch between the communication styles of home and school, noting that discourse practices in various communities differ from those of Western schooling (Barnhardt, 1982; Cazden & John, 1971; Dumont & Wax, 1969; Duranti & Ochs, 1986; Erickson & Mohatt, 1976; Garcia, 1987; Levin, 1990; Tharp, 1989; Vogt, Jordan, & Tharp, 1987). A successful program for coaching mothers of lower socioeconomic status in reading with their preschool children relied on direct instruction in the discourse patterns typical of school: treating the children as conversational peers, asking known-answer (test) questions and praising the children's responses, labeling, providing running commentary, and expanding on the children's vocalization (Edwards, 1989). Understanding local patterns of communication both in and out of school may facilitate school involvement by people whose communities have not traditionally involved this institution.

We think that our observations can aid researchers and educators interested in facilitating the progress in school of non-middle-class children (including cultural minorities in the United States) by elaborating an understanding of patterns of cultural practices that have their own coherence. We avoided a deficit model of difference by studying the practices of the non-middle-class communities that aid children's learning: sensitive assistance in which children's role in learning is active and skilled in ways other than that of middle-class children. We also hope that our analyses will help articulate patterns beyond those we have elaborated.

In like manner, the idea of cross-fertilization has implications for people from communities that have not emphasized skill in learning through observation, taking responsibility for one's own learning, and smooth involvement in group endeavors. Our hopes for the application of our research are not just to facilitate the match between the practices of school and home to enhance non-middle-class children's schooling but also to suggest the utility of fostering keen alertness to ongoing activity, responsibility for managing one's own learning, and participation in groups in schools and middle-class families.

A variety of efforts to reform schools are converging on efforts to change the conception of teaching and learning to a model that may resemble some aspects of learning in the non-middle-class communities. Among these efforts are emphases on school learning as apprenticeship in literacy and on classrooms as communities of readers and writers in which teachers—along with students—engage in integrated projects with visible connections between aspects of the whole and with products of intrinsic interest to class members, working as groups (Kasten, 1992; Moll & Greenberg, 1990; Newman, Griffin, & Cole, 1989; Paradise, 1991; Pewewardy & Bushey, 1992; Tharp & Gallimore, 1988; Wells, Chang, & Maher, 1990).

In his classic account of learning among the Tallensi of Ghana, Fortes (1938/1970, pp. 37–38) critiqued the disembodied form of learning that so commonly occurs in schools:

> It may be observed that even in Western society the principal method of education is by participation. A child repeating the multiplication table is participating in the practical activity appropriate to and defined by the school; but measured by the total social reality it is a factitious activity, a training situation constructed for that purpose. The Tallensi do not make systematic use of training situations. They teach through real situations which children are drawn to participate in because it is expected that they are capable and desirous of mastering the necessary skills. . . . The training situation demands atomic modes of response; the real situation requires organic modes of response. . . . Learning becomes purposive. Every advance in knowledge or skill is pragmatic, directed to achieve a result there and then, as well as adding to a previous level of adequacy.

School reforms that reconstitute children's school activities to involve coherent projects undertaken in academic communities make a major transformation both in discourse practices and relationships between students and teachers and in the conception of how learning of academic topics occurs. They move school practices from dyadic relationships between teachers (conceived as responsible for filling students up with knowledge) and students (who are supposed to be willing receptacles, given some mock excitement, praise, and other motivators) to complex group relationships among class members who learn to take responsibility for contributing to their own learning and to the group's projects. They move schooling from the inculcation of skills out of the context in which they are actually used to communicate or to solve problems to the practice of literate activities in the context of communicating and solving problems. Such restructuring of schools may be motivated both by changes in work requirements—with citizens of the future needing to know how to work in groups (see Heath, 1989)—and by observations that reading and writing are best learned in the context of use.

In our view, all children can benefit from learning to observe keenly and to be responsible for their own learning. We suggest that skill in working with others—as effective and harmonious leaders as well as group members—may be facilitated by the keen observation involved in sharing attention among competing events as well as by facility in engaging in group activity. We have informally observed that master teachers share their attention among a variety of activities as they facilitate students' involvement and learning; this may be a characteristic of leadership that promotes group and individual accomplishment and responsible relationships.

We hope for a future in which the diversity of backgrounds within communities provides children with a flexible facility with—or at least an appreciation of—different patterns of communication that allows them to interact with each other and to provide leadership for their communities. The value of skill in analytic discourse as well as of skilled observation and coordination in groups is clear when we consider the technological as well as social harmony challenges that face us all.

AFTERWORD:
INDEPENDENT ANALYSES OF CULTURAL VARIATIONS AND SIMILARITIES IN SAN PEDRO AND SALT LAKE

Pablo Chavajay

To consider differences between two groups of children in carrying out a task with their mothers it is necessary to take into account the participation and direct intervention of the caregivers because they are the people who guide the children in their first steps in the use of new strategies or reinforce those that are already established. Many of the characteristics of the children from the two groups are a result of the social contexts in which they are embedded; each culture has its own system of norms and values in which the development and interactions of the children evolve. My general comments here are based on viewing videotaped interactions between children and their caregivers in which the children were faced with solving tasks (operating novel objects) under the guidance and with the help of their caregivers.

These observations were made independently by Pablo Chavajay, a native of San Pedro with an advanced degree in psychology from the University of San Carlos in Guatemala City. The observations are based on Chavajay's study of the videotapes of the four oldest toddlers from San Pedro and from Salt Lake (a total of eight toddlers, aged 20–24 months). Chavajay wrote them after spending about 7 months in the United States and after making lengthy written descriptions of the eight videotapes. He was given general guidance regarding the desired level of detail for description by Rogoff and was assisted with translation of the Salt Lake families' English statements (as he also assisted in translating the San Pedro families' Mayan statements). However, the research team was careful not to inform Chavajay of the research questions or of their findings so that his observations could be used as an independent view of a portion of the same data. He knew that we were interested in caregiver-child communication and in how children learn, but we did not specify our questions any further than that. What follows is a condensed translation from a paper that Chavajay wrote in Spanish, with a few elaborations added from an audiorecorded oral presentation.—*B. Rogoff*

THE PROCESS OF INSTRUCTION

The mothers in the two communities differed in the style and strategies that they used to teach and assist their children. At the start of the task (on presentation of the novel objects), the Salt Lake mothers were very expressive emotionally with the goal of attaining and retaining the child's attention, saying, "Wow! Look at *this!*" in a sweet tone of voice. Also, while they were demonstrating the objects, they generally used words to describe how the toy functions. They said "peek-a-boo" and other such words to stimulate the children's interest. The Salt Lake mothers used verbal communication as the principal method of teaching. They varied in the particular content of their explanations and in how much they used verbal interaction, but their teaching was primarily verbal.

Verbal instruction is heavily based on a tradition of formal schooling, which is saturated with instruction that is often unrelated to ongoing activities. Entrance into school conditions and intensifies verbal interaction as the primary and almost the only means of instruction.

The San Pedro mothers were less expressive when teaching their children to operate the toy; they did not need to express additional emotions to get the child's attention. This is not to say that the San Pedro mothers did not use verbal explanation; however, they used a specific pattern that always emphasized to the children that they should observe. At the moment of showing the child how to manipulate the toys they would say, "Look," or, "Did you see?" and afterward they requested, "Now you do it." The instruction of the San Pedro children began with observation, then demonstration with sparse words that always made reference to observation, and finally a request to the child to carry out the process observed.

There were also differences in mother-child assistance during the tasks. When the Salt Lake mothers noticed that their children could not operate the toys adequately, they verbally suggested how the children should manipulate them, usually also with a demonstration involving movements of the hands. They seemed to teach more step by step. While the children tried to manipulate the toys, the parents stimulated them verbally, and, when the children succeeded, they praised them.

After the San Pedro mothers gave the toys to the children, they observed them carefully for a short period and intervened more directly, relating closely with the children. They relied less on verbal explanation, and, if they did use it, their explanation was concise and specific. Generally, they kept watching the children, and, when they noticed that the children were unable to operate the toys, they intervened directly and showed them again as many times as necessary. The San Pedro mothers assisted with an emphasis on observation.

The San Pedro mothers who had attended school longer tended to give more explanation to their children when they were showing the children how to manipulate the toys than did those who had little or no schooling, but they did not lose the specific pattern of instruction, which stands firmly rooted in observation.

MOTHER-CHILD ATTENTION

Although the children of both communities requested their caregivers' assistance in basically the same manner (showing frustration or offering the toy to their parent and waiting for help), there was a difference in the response to the children's requests for help.

San Pedro children generally received their caregivers' help more quickly than did Salt Lake children, who obtained help after insisting that their caregivers, who were often occupied with other activities, pay attention. During conversation with adults, the attention of the Salt Lake mothers was largely centered on the adults with whom they chatted, with the result that often they gave less attention to the children and the children took the liberty of wandering around, changing activities, and going to other people. In San Pedro, mothers did not stop attending to the children while they chatted with the other adults. They continually glanced at their children, with an attention toward the children that remained constant and aware.

Although the mothers from both cultures often attended to more than one thing, helping their children rapidly and often without looking at them while they chatted, this was much more frequent for the San Pedro mothers and children, who engaged in more frequent interaction. It is common in San Pedro for social organization to involve a group of people interacting in a circle with multiple relationships between different people.

The attention that the children gave the adults in both groups differed in the same manner, owing to the differences in the relations of the dyads. The Salt Lake children were more often distant from their parents, perhaps because the parents' attention to them was not constant. The San Pedro children maintained a close relation with their mothers and other caregivers; the attention that they gave the adults was facilitated by the closeness that they maintained with each other, with the greater attention and assistance that they received from their mothers.

The attention of the San Pedro children is related to the social historical process in which the children have developed. In the native Mayan culture, caregivers expect children to begin to learn through observation from birth. Indeed, they always tell the children to observe when they are demonstrating any activity. While parents are working, they also attend to their children and urge the children to pay attention. The children's observation is intensified by the fact that adults do not always give an explanation and that, if they do, it is always after first requesting that the child observe the activity.

The San Pedro children's skill in observation could be seen with some children who at first did not want to play with some of the novel objects and only looked but who later, when none of the adults told them to do so, operated the objects skillfully on their own initiative. There was perhaps greater skill in the operation of complicated novel objects shown by the San Pedro children.

San Pedro caregivers always emphasize to the children to be observant in everyday activities. For example, if a child does not do a good job of work in the field, his father will usually scold him, "Haven't you seen how I showed you?" If small children trip and fall, it is common for their mothers to react by saying, "Don't you have eyes to see where you are walking?" or, "What are your eyes for?" or, "It isn't nighttime and so dark that you cannot see!" Only after making such comments do they help the children up and comfort them.

The different methods of instruction in the two cultures are both valid and result from long social and historical processes. What is emphasized in one culture occurs infrequently in another. This means that both cultures do not take advantage of certain methods of instruction; if both methods of instruction were used in an adequate and balanced way, it would be to the advantage of all. Combining the approaches of both cultures would improve the processes of children's learning.

The differences between the two groups suggest that the caregivers use different strategies and that this has repercussions in the form of the children's learning to solve many of the problems presented in daily life in the social context in which they participate and develop. The methods of instruction have their roots in the complex sociocultural and historical development of each country; in Guatemala, it is notable that the native culture is being heavily influenced by a very different outside world.

REFERENCES

Adamson, L. B., & Bakeman, R. (1982, March). *Encoding videotaped interactions: From counts to context.* Paper presented at the International Conference on Infant Studies, Austin, TX.

Als, H., Tronick, E., & Brazelton, T. B. (1979). Analysis of face-to-face interaction in infant-adult dyads. In M. E. Lamb, S. J. Suomi, & G. R. Stephenson (Eds.), *Social interaction analysis: Methodological issues.* Madison: University of Wisconsin Press.

Altman, I., & Rogoff, B. (1987). World views in psychology: Trait, interactional, organismic, and transactional perspectives. In D. Stokols & I. Altman (Eds.), *Handbook of environmental psychology* (Vol. 1). New York: Wiley.

Balamir-Bazoglu, N. (1982). *Kirsal Turkiye'de egitim ve toplum yapisi* [Rural structure and education in Turkey] (Publication No. T6-0682). Ankara: Middle East Technical University Press.

Barnhardt, C. (1982, December). *Tuning-in: Athabascan teachers and Athabascan students.* Paper presented at the meeting of the American Anthropological Association, Washington, DC.

Benedict, R. (1955). Continuities and discontinuities in cultural conditioning. In M. Mead & M. Wolfenstein (Eds.), *Childhood in contemporary cultures.* Chicago: University of Chicago Press.

Berry, J. W. (1969). On cross-cultural comparability. *International Journal of Psychology, 4,* 119–128.

Blount, B. G. (1972). Parental speech and language acquisition: Some Luo and Samoan examples. *Anthropological Linguistics, 14,* 119–130.

Brazelton, T. B. (1977). Implications of infant development among the Mayan Indians of Mexico. In P. H. Leiderman, S. R. Tulkin, & A. Rosenfeld (Eds.), *Culture and infancy.* New York: Academic.

Brazelton, T. B. (1983). Precursors for the development of emotions in early infancy. In R. Plutchik & H. Kellerman (Eds.), *Emotion: Theory, research, and experience* (Vol. 2). New York: Academic.

Bremme, D., & Erickson, F. (1977). Relationships among verbal and non-verbal classroom behaviors. *Theory into Practice, 5,* 153–161.

Briggs, J. L. (1991). Expecting the unexpected: Canadian Inuit training for an experimental lifestyle. *Ethos, 19,* 259–287.

Cazden, C. B. (1979). *Classroom discourse.* Portsmouth, NH: Heinemann Educational.

Cazden, C. B., Cox, M., Dickinson, D., Steinberg, Z., & Stone, C. (1979). "You all gonna hafta listen": Peer teaching in a primary classroom. In W. A. Collins (Ed.), *Children's language and communication: 12th Annual Minnesota Symposium on Child Psychology.* Hillsdale, NJ: Erlbaum.

Cazden, C. B., & John, V. P. (1971). Learning in American Indian children. In M. L. Wax, S. Diamond, & F. O. Gearing (Eds.), *Anthropological perspectives on education*. New York: Basic.

Cicourel, A. (1974). *Cognitive sociology*. New York: Free Press.

Cole, M. (1985). The zone of proximal development: Where culture and cognition create each other. In J. V. Wertsch (Ed.), *Culture, communication, and cognition: Vygotskian perspectives*. Cambridge: Cambridge University Press.

Cole, M., & Griffin, P. (1980). Cultural amplifiers reconsidered. In D. R. Olson (Ed.), *The social foundations of language and thought*. New York: Norton.

Collier, J., Jr. (1988). Survival at Rough Rock: A historical overview of Rough Rock Demonstration School. *Anthropology and Education Quarterly, 19,* 253–269.

Coy, M. W. (1989). Being what we pretend to be: The usefulness of apprenticeship as a field method. In M. W. Coy (Ed.), *Apprenticeship: From theory to method and back again*. Albany: State University of New York Press.

Dewey, J. (1916). *Democracy and education*. New York: Macmillan.

Deyhle, D. (1991). Empowerment and cultural conflict: Navajo parents and the schooling of their children. *Qualitative Studies in Education, 4,* 277–297.

Dixon, S. D., Levine, R. A., Richman, A., & Brazelton, T. B. (1984). Mother-child interaction around a teaching task: An African-American comparison. *Child Development, 55,* 1252–1264.

Doshi, S. L. (1978). *Processes of tribal unifications and integration*. Delhi: Concept.

Dumont, R., & Wax, M. (1969). Cherokee School Society and the intercultural classroom. *Human Organization, 28,* 219–225.

Duranti, A., & Ochs, E. (1986). Literacy instruction in a Samoan village. In B. B. Schieffelin & P. Gilmore (Eds.), *The acquisition of literacy: Ethnographic perspectives*. Norwood, NJ: Ablex.

Edwards, P. A. (1989). Supporting lower SES mothers' attempts to provide scaffolding for book reading. In J. Allen & J. M. Mason (Eds.), *Risk makers, risk takers, risk breakers*. Portsmouth, NH: Heinemann Educational.

Ellis, S., & Gauvain, M. (1992). Social and cultural influences on children's collaborative interactions. In L. T. Winegar & J. Valsiner (Eds.), *Children's development within social context*. Hillsdale, NJ: Erlbaum.

Erickson, F., & Mohatt, G. (1976). Cultural organization of participation structures in two classrooms of Indian students. In G. Spindler (Ed.), *Doing the ethnography of schooling*. New York: Holt, Rinehart & Winston.

Farran, D. (1982). Mother-child interaction, language development, and the school performance of poverty children. In L. Feagans & D. C. Farran (Eds.), *The language of children reared in poverty*. New York: Academic.

Feinman, S. (1982). Social referencing in infancy. *Merrill-Palmer Quarterly, 28,* 445–470.

Fernald, A. (1984). The perceptual and affective salience of mothers' speech to infants. In L. Feagans, C. Garvey, & R. Golinkoff (Eds.), *The origins and growth of communication*. Norwood, NJ: Ablex.

Field, T. M., Sostek, A. M., Vietze, P., & Leiderman, P. H. (Eds.). (1981). *Culture and early interactions*. Hillsdale, NJ: Erlbaum.

Fortes, M. (1970). Social and psychological aspects of education in Taleland. In J. Middleton (Ed.), *From child to adult*. New York: National History Press. (Original work published 1938)

Fox, B. A. (1988). Interaction as a diagnostic resource in tutoring (Technical Report No. 88-3). Boulder: Institute of Cognitive Science, University of Colorado.

Freed, R. S., & Freed, S. A. (1981). *Enculturation and education in Shanti Nagar* (Anthropological Papers of the American Museum of Natural History, Vol. **57,** Pt. 2). New York: American Museum of Natural History.

Garcia, E. (1987). Interactional style of teachers and parents during bilingual instruction. *Ethnolinguistic Issues in Education,* **21,** 39–51.

Gardner, W. P., & Rogoff, B. (1982). The role of instruction in memory development: Some methodological choices. *Quarterly Newsletter of the Laboratory for Comparative Human Cognition,* **4,** 6–12.

Gaskins, S., & Lucy, J. A. (1987, May). *The role of children in the production of adult culture: A Yucatec case.* Paper presented at the meeting of the American Ethnological Society, San Antonio, TX.

Gelfand, D. M., & Hartmann, D. P. (1975). *Child behavior analysis and therapy.* New York: Pergamon.

Gerez, T. de. (1984). *My song is a piece of jade: Poems of ancient Mexico in English and Spanish.* Boston: Little, Brown.

Goetz, J. P., & LeCompte, M. D. (1984). *Ethnography and qualitative design in educational research.* Orlando, FL: Academic.

Göncü, A., Mistry, J., & Mosier, C. (in progress). *Cultural variation in toddlers' play.*

Goody, E. N. (1978). Towards a theory of questions. In E. N. Goody (Ed.), *Questions and politeness.* Cambridge: Cambridge University Press.

Government of Rajasthan. (1988). *Draft annual plan for tribal development in Rajasthan, 1989–90* (Vol. **1**). Udaipur: Tribal Area Development Department, Government of Rajasthan.

Green, J., & Wallat, C. (1979). What is an instructional context? An exploratory analysis of conversational shifts across time. In O. K. Garnica & M. I. King (Eds.), *Language, children, and society.* Oxford: Pergamon.

Greenfield, P. M. (1984). A theory of the teacher in the learning activities of everyday life. In B. Rogoff & J. Lave (Eds.), *Everyday cognition: Its development in social context.* Cambridge, MA: Harvard University Press.

Greenfield, P. M., & Lave, J. (1982). Cognitive aspects of informal education. In D. Wagner & H. Stevenson (Eds.), *Cultural perspectives on child development.* San Francisco: Freeman.

Grossmann, K. E. (1981, April). *Infant and social environmental interaction: Epistemological considerations behind the ethological approach.* Paper presented at the meeting of the Society for Research in Child Development, Boston.

Guba, E. G., & Lincoln, Y. S. (1982). Epistemological and methodological bases of naturalistic inquiry. *Educational Communication and Technology Journal,* **30,** 233–252.

Gundlach, R., McLane, J. B., Stott, F. M., & McNamee, G. D. (1985). The social foundations of children's early writing development. In M. Farr (Ed.), *Advances in writing research* (Vol. **1**). Norwood, NJ: Ablex.

Haight, W. (1991, April). *Parents' ideas about pretend play.* Paper presented at the meeting of the Society for Research in Child Development, Seattle.

Harkness, S., & Super, C. M. (1977). Why African children are so hard to test. In L. L. Adler (Ed.), *Issues in cross-cultural research. Annals of the New York Academy of Sciences,* **285,** 326–331.

Heath, S. B. (1982). What no bedtime story means: Narrative skills at home and school. *Language in Society,* **11,** 49–76.

Heath, S. B. (1983). *Ways with words: Language, life, and work in communities and classrooms.* Cambridge: Cambridge University Press.

Heath, S. B. (1989). The learner as cultural member. In M. L. Rice & R. L. Schiefelbusch (Eds.), *The teachability of language.* Baltimore: Paul H. Brookes.

Henry, J. (1955). Culture, education, and communications theory. In G. D. Spindler (Ed.), *Education and anthropology*. Stanford, CA: Stanford University Press.

Hilger, Sister M. I. (1966). *Field guide to the ethnological study of child life*. New Haven, CT: Human Relations Area Files Press.

Hoff-Ginsberg, E. (1991). Mother-child conversation in different social classes and communicative settings. *Child Development, 62*, 782–796.

Howard, A. (1970). *Learning to be Rotuman*. New York: Teachers College Press.

Huberty, C. J., & Morris, J. D. (1989). Multivariate analysis vs. multiple univariate analyses. *Psychological Bulletin, 105*, 302–308.

Jacob, E. (1987). Qualitative research traditions: A review. *Review of Educational Research, 57*, 1–50.

John-Steiner, V. (1984). Learning styles among Pueblo children. *Quarterly Newsletter of the Laboratory of Comparative Human Cognition, 6*, 57–62.

Jordan, C. (1977, February). *Maternal teaching, peer teaching, and school adaptation in an urban Hawaiian population*. Paper presented at the meeting of the Society for Cross-Cultural Research, East Lansing, MI.

Kasten, W. C. (1992). Bridging the horizon: American Indian beliefs and whole language learning. *Anthropology and Education Quarterly, 23*, 108–119.

Kenyatta, J. (1953). *Facing Mount Kenya: The tribal life of the Gikuyu*. London: Secker & Warburg.

Kojima, H. (1986). Child rearing concepts as a belief-value system of the society and the individual. In H. Stevenson, H. Azuma, & K. Hakuta (Eds.), *Child development and education in Japan*. New York: Freeman.

Kreppner, K., Paulsen, S., & Schuetze, Y. (1982). Infant and family development: From triads to tetrads. *Human Development, 25*, 373–391.

Laboratory of Comparative Human Cognition. (1983). Culture and cognitive development. In W. Kessen (Ed.), P. H. Mussen (Series Ed.), *Handbook of child psychology: Vol. 1. History, theory, and methods*. New York: Wiley.

Lamphere, L. (1977). *To run after them: Cultural and social bases of cooperation in a Navajo community*. Tucson: University of Arizona Press.

Lave, J., & Wenger, E. (1991). *Situated learning: Legitimate peripheral participation*. Cambridge: Cambridge University Press.

LeCompte, M. D., & Goetz, J. P. (1982). Problems of reliability and validity in ethnographic research. *Review of Educational Research, 52*, 31–60.

Lee, D. D. (1976). *Valuing the self: What we can learn from other cultures*. Englewood Cliffs, NJ: Prentice-Hall.

Leiderman, P. H., Tulkin, S. R., & Rosenfeld, A. (Eds.). (1977). *Culture and infancy: Variations in the human experience*. New York: Academic.

Leont'ev, A. N. (1981). The problem of activity in psychology. In J. V. Wertsch (Ed.), *The concept of activity in Soviet psychology*. Armonk, NY: Sharpe.

Levin, P. F. (1990). Culturally contextualized apprenticeship: Teaching and learning through helping in Hawaiian families. *Quarterly Newsletter of the Laboratory for Comparative Human Cognition, 12*, 80–86.

Luria, A. R. (1987). Afterword to the Russian edition. In R. W. Rieber & A. S. Carton (Eds.), *The collected works of L. S. Vygotsky: Vol. 1. Problems of general psychology*. New York: Plenum.

Maim, R. S. (1978). Religious attributes of Bhils. *Tribe* (Maniklal Verma Tribal Research and Training Institute, Udaipur, Rajasthan), *10*, 109–122.

Mann, K. (1988). *Status of Bhil women—a study of continuity and change*. New Delhi: Discovery.

Martini, M., & Kirkpatrick, J. (1981). Early interactions in the Marquesas Islands. In T. M. Fields, A. M. Sostek, P. Vietze, & P. H. Leiderman (Eds.), *Culture and early interactions*. Hillsdale, NJ: Erlbaum.

McDermott, R. P., Gospodinoff, K., & Aron, J. (1978). Criteria for an ethnographically adequate description of concerted activities and their contexts. *Semiotica, 24,* 245–275.

Mehan, H. (1979). *Learning lessons.* Cambridge, MA: Harvard University Press.

Mehan, H., et al. (1976). *Texts of classroom discourse* (Report No. 67a). La Jolla: Center for Human Information Processing, University of California, San Diego.

Mehan, H., & Riel, M. M. (in press). Teachers' and students' instructional strategies. In L. L. Adler (Ed.), *Issues in cross-cultural research.* New York: Academic.

Michaels, S., & Cazden, C. B. (1986). Teacher/child collaboration as oral preparation for literacy. In B. B. Schieffelin & P. Gilmore (Eds.), *The acquisition of literacy: Ethnographic perspectives.* Norwood, NJ: Ablex.

Miles, M. B., & Huberman, A. M. (1984). *Qualitative data analysis.* Beverly Hills, CA: Sage.

Mistry, J., Göncü, A., & Rogoff, B. (1988, April). *Cultural variations in role relations in the socialization of toddlers.* Paper presented at the International Conference of Infant Studies, Washington, DC.

Moll, L. C., & Greenberg, J. B. (1990). Creating zones of possibilities: Combining social contexts for instruction. In L. C. Moll (Ed.), *Vygotsky and education: Instructional implications and applications of sociohistorical psychology.* Cambridge: Cambridge University Press.

Moore, D. T. (1981). Discovering the pedagogy of experience. *Harvard Educational Review, 2,* 286–300.

Morelli, G., Rogoff, B., & Angelillo, C. (1992, September). *Cultural variation in young children's opportunities for involvement in adult activities.* Paper presented at the Conference for Socio-Cultural Research, Madrid.

Morelli, G. A., Rogoff, B., Oppenheim, D., & Goldsmith, D. (1992). Cultural variation in infants' sleeping arrangements: Questions of independence. *Developmental Psychology, 28,* 604–613.

Mosier, C., Rogoff, B., & Chavajay, P. (1992, September). *Uniqueness of infants' role in the family: Cultural issues of independence and interdependence.* Paper presented at the meeting of the Society for Socio-Cultural Studies, Madrid.

Nash, M. (1967). *Machine age Maya.* Chicago: University of Chicago Press.

Newman, D., Griffin, P., & Cole, M. (1989). *The construction zone: Working for cognitive change in school.* Cambridge: Cambridge University Press.

Newson, J. (1977). An intersubjective approach to the systematic description of mother-infant interaction. In H. R. Schaffer (Ed.), *Studies in mother-infant interaction.* New York: Academic.

Niehardt, J. G. (1932). *Black Elk speaks.* New York: Pocket.

Ochs, E. (1988). *Culture and language development: Language acquisition and language socialization in a Samoan village.* Cambridge: Cambridge University Press.

Ochs, E., & Schieffelin, B. B. (1984). Language acquisition and socialization: Three developmental stories and their implications. In R. Schweder & R. LeVine (Eds.), *Culture and its acquisition.* Chicago: University of Chicago Press.

Panel on Youth of the President's Science Advisory Committee. (1974). *Youth: Transition to adulthood.* Chicago: University of Chicago Press.

Paradise, R. (1991). El conocimiento cultural en el aula: Niños indígenas y su orientación hacia la observación [Cultural knowledge in the classroom: Indigenous children and their orientation toward observation]. *Infancia y Aprendizaje, 55,* 73–85.

Peak, L. (1986). Training learning skills and attitudes in Japanese early educational settings. In W. Fowler (Ed.), *Early experience and the development of competence.* San Francisco: Jossey-Bass.

Pepper, S. C. (1942). *World hypotheses: A study in evidence.* Berkeley: University of California Press.

Pewewardy, C., & Bushey, M. (1992). A family of learners and storytellers. *Native Peoples,* **5,** 56–60.

Richman, A. L., LeVine, R. A., New, R. S., Howrigan, G. A., Welles-Nystrom, B., & LeVine, S. E. (1988). Maternal behavior to infants in five cultures. In R. A. LeVine, P. M. Miller, & M. M. West (Eds.), *Parental behavior in diverse societies.* San Francisco: Jossey-Bass.

Richman, A. L., Miller, P. M., & Solomon, M. J. (1988). The socialization of infants in suburban Boston. In R. A. LeVine, P. M. Miller, & M. M. West (Eds.), *Parental behavior in diverse societies.* San Francisco: Jossey-Bass.

Rogoff, B. (1976). *A life cycle ethnography: San Pedro la Laguna, a Highland Maya community.* Unpublished manuscript, Harvard University and the Institute of Nutrition of Central America and Panama.

Rogoff, B. (1981a). Adults and peers as agents of socialization: A Highland Guatemalan profile. *Ethos,* **9,** 18–36.

Rogoff, B. (1981b). Schooling and the development of cognitive skills. In H. C. Triandis & A. Heron (Eds.), *Handbook of cross-cultural psychology* (Vol. 4). Rockleigh, NJ: Allyn & Bacon.

Rogoff, B. (1982a). Integrating context and cognitive development. In M. E. Lamb & A. L. Brown (Eds.), *Advances in developmental psychology* (Vol. 2). Hillsdale, NJ: Erlbaum.

Rogoff, B. (1982b). Mode of instruction and memory test performance. *International Journal of Behavioral Development,* **5,** 33–48.

Rogoff, B. (1986). Adult assistance of children's learning. In T. E. Raphael (Ed.), *The contexts of school based literacy.* New York: Random.

Rogoff, B. (1990). *Apprenticeship in thinking: Cognitive development in social context.* New York: Oxford University Press.

Rogoff, B. (in press). Observing sociocultural activity on three planes: Participatory appropriation, guided participation, apprenticeship. In A. Alvarez, P. del Rio, & J. V. Wertsch (Eds.), *Perspectives on sociocultural research.* Cambridge: Cambridge University Press.

Rogoff, B., & Gardner, W. P. (1984). Adult guidance of cognitive development. In B. Rogoff & J. Lave (Eds.), *Everyday cognition: Its development in social context.* Cambridge, MA: Harvard University Press.

Rogoff, B., & Gauvain, M. (1986). A method for the analysis of patterns, illustrated with data on mother-child instructional interaction. In J. Valsiner (Ed.), *The role of the individual subject in scientific psychology.* New York: Plenum.

Rogoff, B., Gauvain, M., & Ellis, S. (1984). Development viewed in its cultural context. In M. H. Bornstein & M. E. Lamb (Eds.), *Developmental psychology.* Hillsdale, NJ: Erlbaum.

Rogoff, B., Mistry, J., Göncü, A., & Mosier, C. (1991). Cultural variation in the role relations of toddlers and their families. In M. H. Bornstein (Ed.), *Cultural approaches to parenting.* Hillsdale, NJ: Erlbaum.

Rogoff, B., Mosier, C., Mistry, J., & Göncü, A. (in press). Toddlers' guided participation with their caregivers in cultural activity. In E. Forman, N. Minick, & A. Stone (Eds.), *Contexts for learning: Sociocultural dynamics in children's development.* New York: Oxford University Press.

Rogoff, B., Sellers, M. J., Pirotta, S., Fox, N., & White, S. H. (1975). Age of assignment of roles and responsibilities to children: A cross-cultural survey. *Human Development*, **18**, 353–369.

Ruddle, K., & Chesterfield, R. (1978). Traditional skill training and labor in rural societies. *Journal of Developing Areas*, **12**, 389–398.

Schieffelin, B. B. (1991). *The give and take of everyday life: Language socialization of Kaluli children*. Cambridge: Cambridge University Press.

Schieffelin, B. B., & Eisenberg, A. R. (1984). Cultural variation in children's conversations. In R. Schiefelbusch & J. Pickar (Eds.), *The acquisition of communicative competence*. Baltimore: University Park Press.

Scribner, S. (1974). Developmental aspects of categorized recall in a West African society. *Cognitive Psychology*, **6**, 475–494.

Scribner, S., & Cole, M. (1973). Cognitive consequences of formal and informal education. *Science*, **182**, 553–559.

Scribner, S., & Cole, M. (1981). *The psychology of literacy*. Cambridge, MA: Harvard University Press.

Shotter, J. (1978). The cultural context of communication studies: Theoretical and methodological issues. In A. Lock (Ed.), *Action, gesture, and symbol: The emergence of language*. New York: Academic.

Sorce, J. F., Emde, R. N., Campos, J., & Klinnert, M. D. (1985). Maternal emotional signaling: Its effect on the visual cliff behavior of 1-year-olds. *Developmental Psychology*, **21**, 195–200.

Sorenson, E. R. (1979). Early tactile communication and the patterning of human organization: A New Guinea case study. In M. Bullowa (Ed.), *Before speech: The beginning of interpersonal communication*. Cambridge: Cambridge University Press.

Sostek, A. M., Vietze, P., Zaslow, M., Kreiss, L., van der Waals, F., & Rubenstein, D. (1981). Social context in caregiver-infant interaction: A film study of Fais and the United States. In T. M. Field, A. M. Sostek, P. Vietze, & P. H. Leiderman (Eds.), *Culture and early interactions*. Hillsdale, NJ: Erlbaum.

Taylor, D. (1983). *Family literacy*. Portsmouth, NH: Heinemann Educational.

Tharp, R. G. (1989). Psychocultural variables and constants: Effects on teaching and learning in schools. *American Psychologist*, **44**, 349–359.

Tharp, R. G., & Gallimore, R. (1988). *Rousing minds to life: Teaching, learning, and schooling in social context*. Cambridge: Cambridge University Press.

Trevarthen, C. (1988). Universal co-operative motives: How infants begin to know the language and culture of their parents. In G. Jahoda & I. M. Lewis (Eds.), *Acquiring culture: Cross-cultural studies in child development*. London: Croom Helm.

Trevarthen, C., Hubley, P., & Sheeran, L. (1975). Les activités innés du nourrisson [Innate activities of the newborn]. *La Recherche*, **6**, 447–458.

Tukey, J. W. (1977). *Exploratory data analysis*. Reading, MA: Addison-Wesley.

Uzgiris, I. C., & Fafouti-Milenkovic, M. (1985). Over het verband tussen methode en theorie bij onderzoek naarouder-kind interaktie [The tie between methodology and theory in the study of parent-infant interaction]. In J. deWit, H. J. Groenendaal, & J. M. vanMeel (Eds.), *Psychologen over het kind* [Psychology of the child] (Vol. 8). Lisse: Swets & Zeitlinger.

Vogt, L. A., Jordan, C., & Tharp, R. G. (1987). Explaining school failure, producing school success: Two cases. *Anthropology and Education Quarterly*, **18**, 276–286.

Vygotsky, L. S. (1978). *Mind in society: The development of higher psychological processes*. Cambridge, MA: Harvard University Press.

Ward, M. C. (1971). *Them children: A study in language learning*. New York: Holt, Rinehart & Winston.

Watson-Gegeo, K. A., & Gegeo, D. W. (1986a). Communicative routines in Kwara'ae children's language socialization (Final report). Washington, DC: National Science Foundation.

Watson-Gegeo, K. A., & Gegeo, D. W. (1986b). The social world of Kwara'ae children: Acquisition of language and values. In J. Cook-Gumperz, W. Corsaro, & J. Streeck (Eds.), *Children's worlds and children's language*. The Hague: Mouton.

Weisner, T. S., & Gallimore, R. (1977). My brother's keeper: Child and sibling caretaking. *Current Anthropology, 18,* 169–190.

Wellman, B., & Sim, S. (1990, February). Integrating textual and statistical methods in the social sciences. *Cultural Anthropology Newsletter, 2,* 1–3, 10–11.

Wells, G., Chang, G. L. M., & Maher, A. (1990). Creating classroom communities of literate thinkers. In S. Sharan (Ed.), *Cooperative learning: Theory and research*. New York: Praeger.

Werner, H. (1954). *Comparative psychology of mental development*. New York: International Universities Press.

Wertsch, J. V. (1979). From social interaction to higher psychological processes. *Human Development, 22,* 1–22.

Wertsch, J. V. (1984). The zone of proximal development: Some conceptual issues. In B. Rogoff & J. V. Wertsch (Eds.), *Children's learning in the "zone of proximal development."* San Francisco: Jossey-Bass.

Whiting, B. B., & Edwards, C. P. (1988). *Children of different worlds: The formation of social behavior*. Cambridge, MA: Harvard University Press.

Whiting, J. W. M. (1981). Environmental constraints on infant care practices. In R. H. Munroe, R. L. Munroe, & B. B. Whiting (Eds.), *Handbook of cross-cultural human development*. New York: Garland.

Whiting, J. W. M., Child, I. L., Lambert, W. W., Fischer, A. M., Fischer, J. L., Nydegger, C., Nydegger, W., Maretzki, H., Maretzki, T., Minturn, L., Romney, A. K., & Romney, R. (1966). *Field guide for a study of socialization*. New York: Wiley.

ACKNOWLEDGMENTS

This research began while we were all at the University of Utah; we would like to acknowledge the support and fertile ground provided by our colleagues at Utah and the early guidance of Beatrice Whiting and Benjamin and Lois Paul. We are grateful to several sources of funding that contributed to various phases of gathering data, analyzing results, and writing the *Monograph:* the National Institute of Mental Health (Small Grants), the MacArthur Foundation, the Spencer Foundation, and the University of Utah Research Committee.

We appreciate the comments and assistance of Bill Buxton, Pablo Chavajay, Jamie Germond, Denise Goldsmith, Nancy Bell, Alan Fogel, Wendy Haight, Shirley Brice Heath, Robert LeVine, and Roger Bakeman. Also, the assistance of Marta Navichoc Cotuc, Pablo Chavajay, Jamie Germond, Kathy Lewkowitz, and Amy Urbanek in preparing Chapter IV, of Suniti Sundaresen, Bhagwati Behen, and Daya Saxena in the data collection underlying Chapter V, and of Recai Coskun, Esam Saraf, and Filiz Kücüktunc in the data collection underlying Chapter VI is greatly appreciated. Most of all, we are indebted to the families involved in this research for welcoming us into their homes and for their help in illuminating processes of children's development.

Please address correspondence to Barbara Rogoff, Psychology Department, Kerr Hall, University of California, Santa Cruz, CA 95064.

THE STUDY OF CULTURAL ACTIVITY:
MOVING TOWARD MULTIPLE APPROACHES IN
RESEARCH ON CHILD DEVELOPMENT

Shirley Brice Heath

> Nobody can offer a blueprint on how an intermediate generation
> can help ready the less mature for life in an unforeseeably chang-
> ing world. (Bruner, 1976, p. 59)

Just as there can be no blueprint for socialization, so there can be none
for studying all the processes by which the less mature learn to learn, to
become cultural members of their own enculturating group. It is promising
that current work that establishes activity, activity settings, and participants
at the center of studies of individuals interacting in learning draws from
several sets of blueprints. Hence, the design, structure, and foundation of
the resulting work offer useful perspectives for studying children's development across cultures and situations.

The work of Barbara Rogoff, Jayanthi Mistry, Artin Göncü, and Christine Mosier breaks ground for the field of child development in ways that
respect the concerns of psychologists and yet take up new directions from
other disciplines, particularly anthropology. The data from several cultures
that vary by occupation, class, and geographic region should be of great
interest to all those who now worry increasingly about cultural differences
and ways to capture these without falling into simplistic stereotypes. The
theoretical and conceptual underpinnings of the work in guided participation are well explained and grounded in supporting theory from other
psychologists, such as Vygotsky, and also anthropologists, whose work from
several cultures echoes the findings here.

This remarkable study is notable for its care in not overextending findings, its attention to the explication and the limitations of methods, and its precision in definition. For those who struggle to understand learning and its environments in an increasingly complex and political environment fragmented around such concepts as "multiculturalism," this *Monograph* should become a handbook to guide researchers in ways to keep individual, interpersonal, and cultural processes simultaneously in focus. It does its best methodologically and does not fall into the sort of self-discrediting that often weakens work responding to current questions of different epistemologies by casting strong doubts on science and especially forms of ethnographic documentation, especially narratives.

This volume offers strong findings and statements regarding universals and variations in guided participation. It should therefore serve as a constant reminder that the mainstream bias toward interactions that include verbal communication must give way to ensure attention to distal arrangements of activity and nonverbal signals of attention to visual and kinesthetic cues from the environment to the learner. Yet another value of this volume is its care to step away from strong tendencies in the social sciences to dichotomize outcomes. Readers cannot go away from this volume with the sense that all those of the middle class socialize children in one way while the socialization practices of other classes may be lumped into one "other" set of practices. This volume shows again and again, by systematic, well-explicated methods, the intricate interactions of various pieces of context that become salient or remain out of awareness in parent-child interactions. Only because researchers in each site either had extensive experience in the community or had worked closely with a local resident educated in the social sciences were they able to contextualize their videotapes and interviews. Knowing something of the range of cultural behaviors of the groups studied enabled the researchers to embed their interpretations of their findings within such subtle cultural values as attention management, individualism, and self-reliance in synch with those of a group engaged in a joint activity. Their videotapings represent a close and focused look at certain activities identified as appropriate for such recording *precisely* because of the researchers' access to more thorough and far-reaching knowledge of the settings. Thus, this one slice of adult-child interaction for analysis was validated in large part by the grounding it achieved within the cultural context. These authors would never say that they see a single videotaped episode of mother-child interaction *without* such grounding as *ethnographic*.

Interest in this volume should come not only from those in early child development but also from several groups that do not usually read this *Monograph* series. For example, those who have followed the controversy regarding the effects of schools and schooling will find this volume very relevant for those debates. Others who have tried to break the "great divide" between quantitative and qualitative research will also find this work a model. For classes in socialization, research methods, and the psychology of learning, this will be an excellent choice of text.

Given the breadth of audience that may find this work of interest, it may be useful to speculate on ways that researchers especially interested in the learning of older children and of adolescents might take some lessons on research methods and theories of learning away from this volume. This volume echoes many of the methodological and ideological concerns over past research on learning and development expressed by anthropologists such as Lave and Wenger (1991) and others drawn to "cultural psychology" (e.g., contributors in Shweder & LeVine, 1984, and Stigler, Shweder, & Herdt, 1990). Yet Rogoff et al. go further toward explication of methods that might follow from some of these concerns than have most social scientists who have attempted to bring anthropology and psychology closer together.

In at least three ways, this volume carries messages highly relevant for scholars attempting to study the learning of older children. First, the work here should encourage researchers to attend far more carefully to ways that nonverbal symbolic acts (such as gaze, touch, timing, and spatial use cues and gestures) integrate learners across levels of skills and knowledge into activities. Such incorporation often comes through role shifting for older children so that following verbal orders from elders or experts is subverted by being diverted to a mode of peer play. In this way, youths sometimes create public performances with their peers that appear to have little to do with what adults want them to learn but may incorporate far more complex and multiply-mediated types of learning than the "lesson" or directives that might be verbally given by elders (cf. Goodwin, 1990).

A second direction from this work for those who study older children is a focus on issues such as responsibility in learning and maintaining awareness on several levels simultaneously. Cultural activities carry opportunities in which individuals in interaction with others, through mediated and direct experience of their environment, self-select and create their enculturative structures and styles. All learners have some decision-making role in determining whether they jump right into new situations or stand back and watch. Similarly, their styled displays of learning may include clowning through a trial-and-error situation or asking for verbal clarification and repeated demonstration before giving any evidence of learning or of even wanting to take a role in a new situation. Such adaptations—both individual and group—indicate types and levels of responsibility for self-identity in learning and orientations to the future and one's role in possible futures. Although this volume does not explicitly deal with the different perceptions of future worlds held by the cultural groups studied, much can be inferred about the extent to which parents hold their children accountable for certain types of learning that the elders believe relevant for coming adulthood.

These future worldviews potentially influence orientations to learning that persist throughout the life span for individuals and thus influence the types of groups from and with whom individuals choose to learn.

Inseparable from responsibility in learning is the matter of attending to multiple experiential processes, mediated means, and attendant affective dimensions. Most studies of the learning of older children have ignored the multiple sides of learning and have centered on single tasks, measuring specific skills across brief exposures to teaching or opportunities to practice. However, recent studies strongly influenced by the work of Vygotsky have stressed the monitoring of context and mediation of tools, along with self-directed speech and cooperative play in performance groups that work together simultaneously (Moll, 1990, esp. pt. 2; Tharp & Gallimore, 1988).

A third effect of this work—perhaps more indirect than the previous two—should encourage the studies of those who have emphasized detailed attention to oral and written language and their roles in both a first-learning experience and the repetition and buildup of such initial learning in new situations. The pragmatics of any occasion will play a major role in shaping indexicality and figure-and-ground relations, which in turn influence perceptual salience. Enculturation helps determine the readiness of learners to pick up on that salience and the designation of roles of direct and mediated experiences in doing so. All natural languages have deictics—ways of pointing out or demonstrating what is being referenced in language. Caregivers, experts, and teachers, especially when using objects in their instruction, rely heavily on encoding information and cuing levels of attention through deictics. When what is being attended to by learners is nonverbal symbolic information or peer language, for example, adults may need to move from presentative deictics to those that are expressive, directive, or the like to channel perception toward adult-preferred foci of learning (Hanks, 1992). Current knowledge tells us little about how spatial and time cues that are nonverbal interact with verbal messages to foreground certain information or skills.

Much has recently been written and said in conferences about both the need to bring anthropology and psychology closer together and the risks involved in doing so. This *Monograph* should play a major role in future discussions and papers centered around the topics of socialization, learning, and enculturation. Anthropologists and such psychologists as the authors of this volume want more of the linkage of the two disciplines than acknowledgment by psychologists of cross-cultural variation in developmental processes and variation. (For a discussion of similar points, see Harkness, 1992.) They want increasing concern with *culture*, a concern that will include "all of the internalized derivatives of experience distributed among the members of a population . . . who to a large extent process culturally informed

She is the author of *Ways with Words: Language, Life and Work in Communities and Classrooms* (1983) and coauthor (with Shelby A. Wolf) of *The Braid of Literature: Children's Worlds of Reading* (1992). Her current research interests include learning in peer activities among adolescents.

STATEMENT OF EDITORIAL POLICY

The *Monographs* series is intended as an outlet for major reports of developmental research that generate authoritative new findings and use these to foster a fresh and/or better-integrated perspective on some conceptually significant issue or controversy. Submissions from programmatic research projects are particularly welcome; these may consist of individually or group-authored reports of findings from some single large-scale investigation or of a sequence of experiments centering on some particular question. Multiauthored sets of independent studies that center on the same underlying question can also be appropriate; a critical requirement in such instances is that the various authors address common issues and that the contribution arising from the set as a whole be both unique and substantial. In essence, irrespective of how it may be framed, any work that contributes significant data and/or extends developmental thinking will be taken under editorial consideration.

Submissions should contain a minimum of 80 manuscript pages (including tables and references); the upper limit of 150–175 pages is much more flexible (please submit four copies; a copy of every submission and associated correspondence is deposited eventually in the archives of the SRCD). Neither membership in the Society for Research in Child Development nor affiliation with the academic discipline of psychology are relevant; the significance of the work in extending developmental theory and in contributing new empirical information is by far the most crucial consideration. Because the aim of the series is not only to advance knowledge on specialized topics but also to enhance cross-fertilization among disciplines or subfields, it is important that the links between the specific issues under study and larger questions relating to developmental processes emerge as clearly to the general reader as to specialists on the given topic.

Potential authors who may be unsure whether the manuscript they are planning would make an appropriate submission are invited to draft an outline of what they propose and send it to the Editor for assessment.

This mechanism, as well as a more detailed description of all editorial policies, evaluation processes, and format requirements, is given in the "Guidelines for the Preparation of *Monographs* Submissions," which can be obtained by writing to the Editor designate, Rachel K. Clifton, Department of Psychology, University of Massachusetts, Amherst, MA 01003.

DATE DUE
